27 COLORING PAGES

GOLF COLORING BOOK

FOR KIDS ALL AGES

SCAN THE QR CODE !
VISIT OUR AUTHOR PAGE ON AMAZON.COM AND CHECK OTHER COLORING PAGES!

Scan Me!

All rights Reserved. No part of this book may be used or reproduced in any manner whatsever without written permission except in the case of brief quotations embodied in critical articles and interviews

By Juliana Rentell

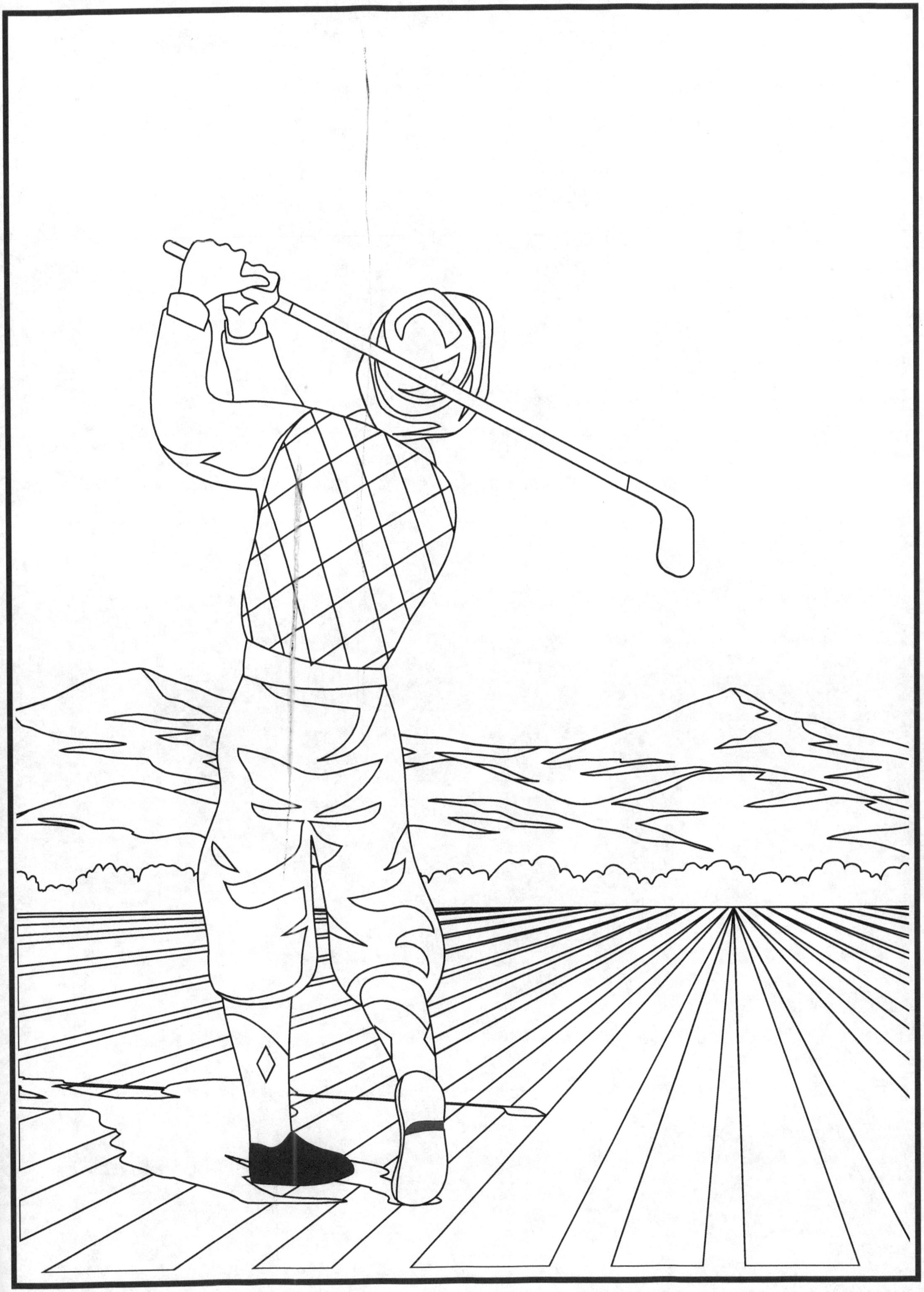

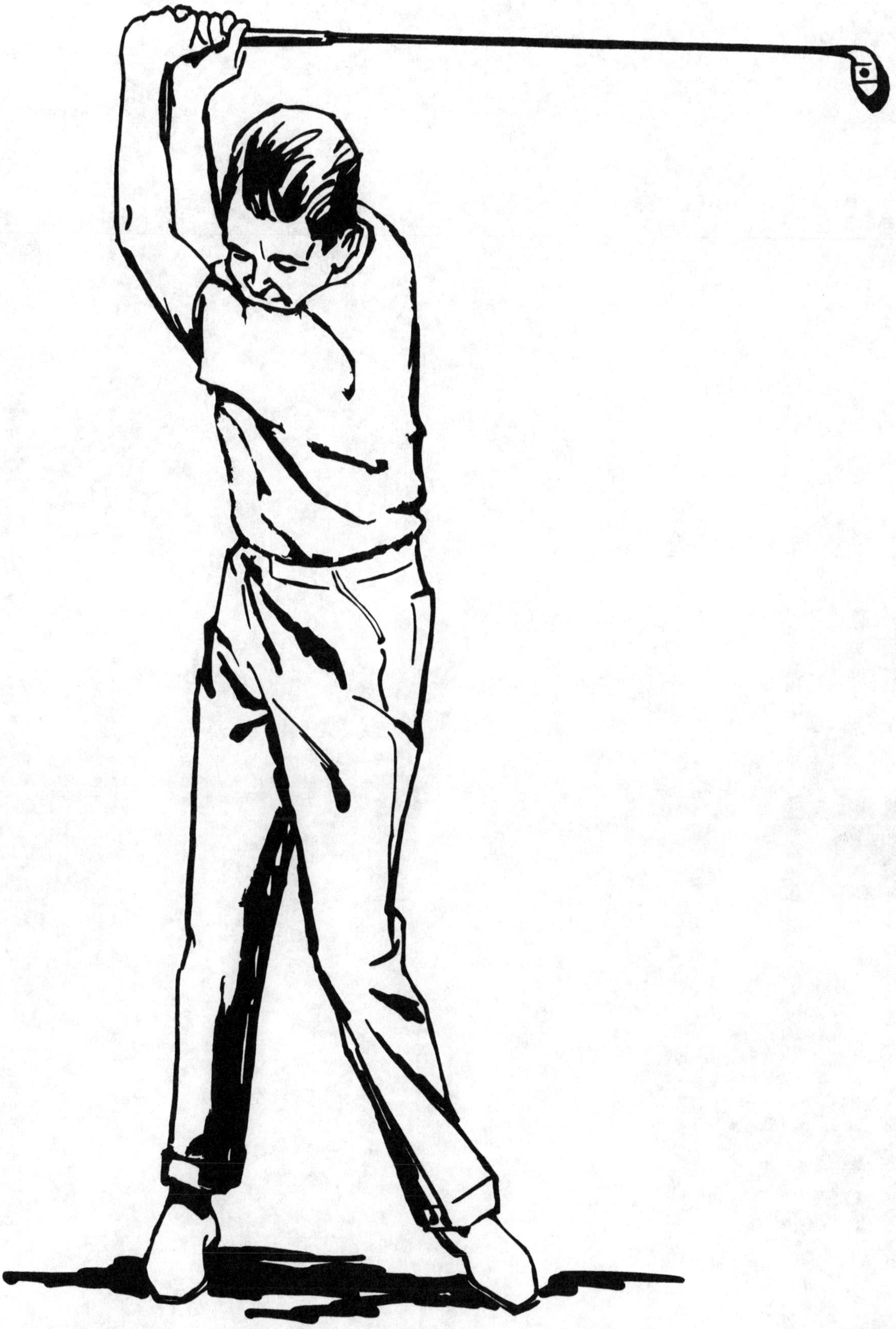

GOLF

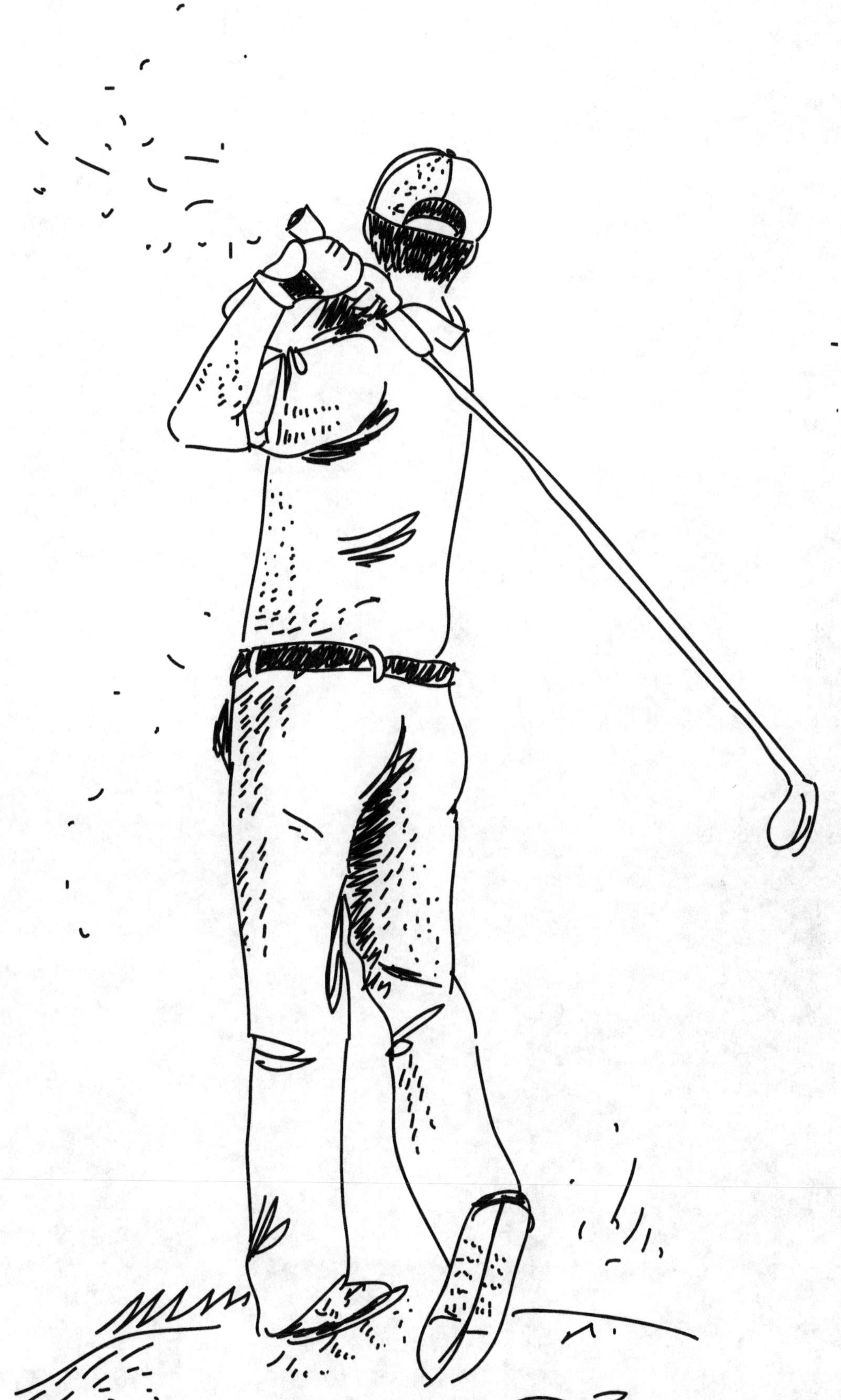

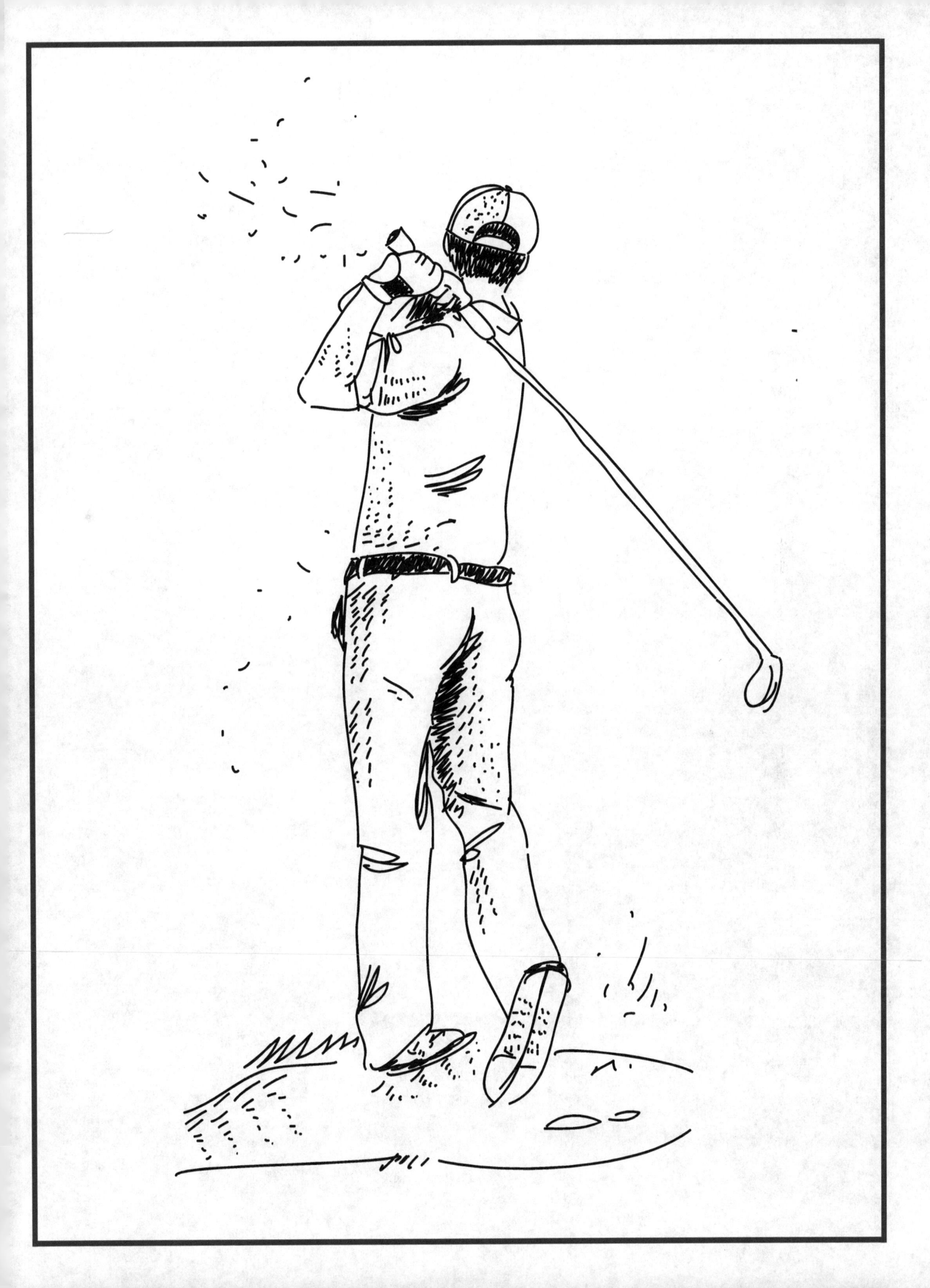

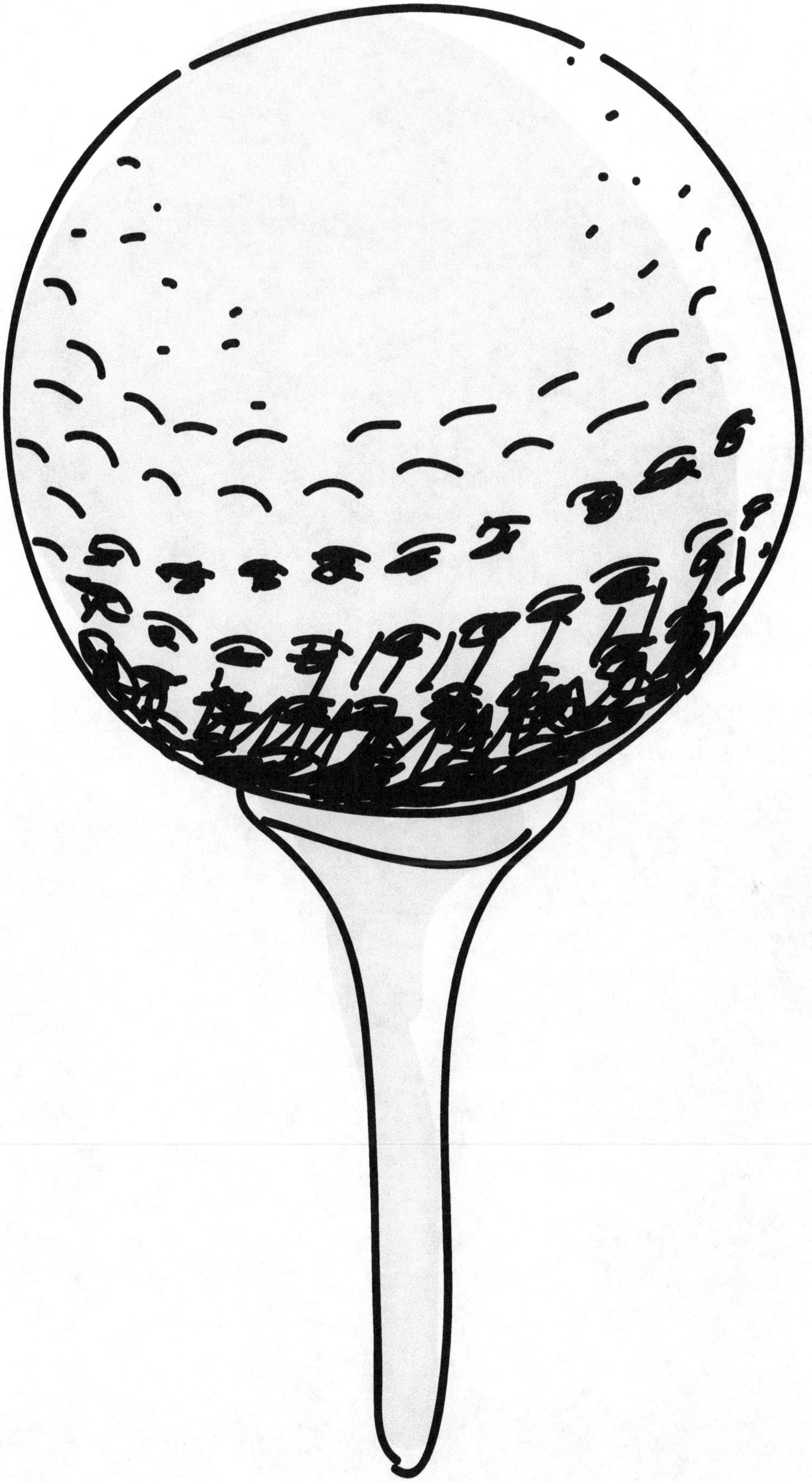

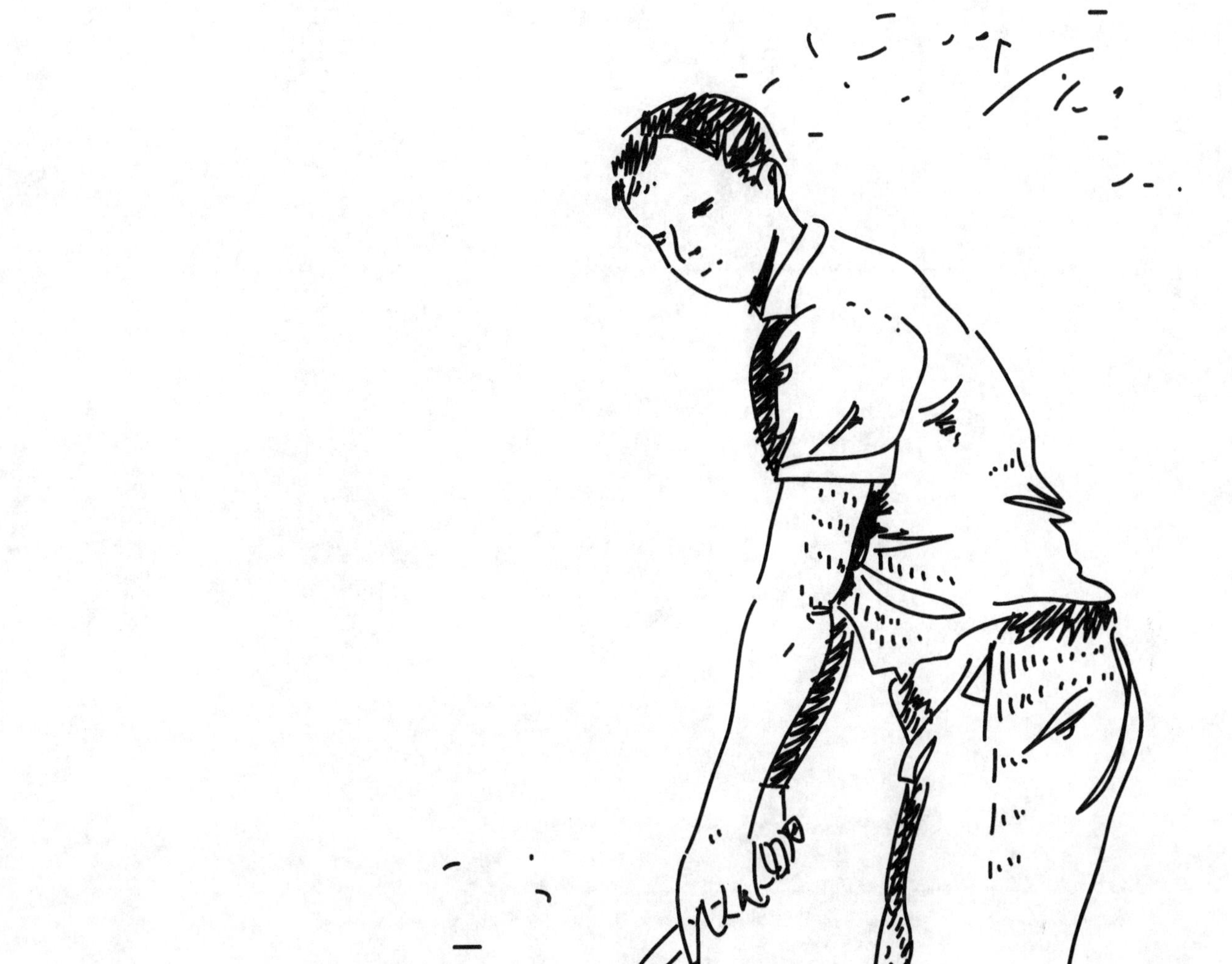

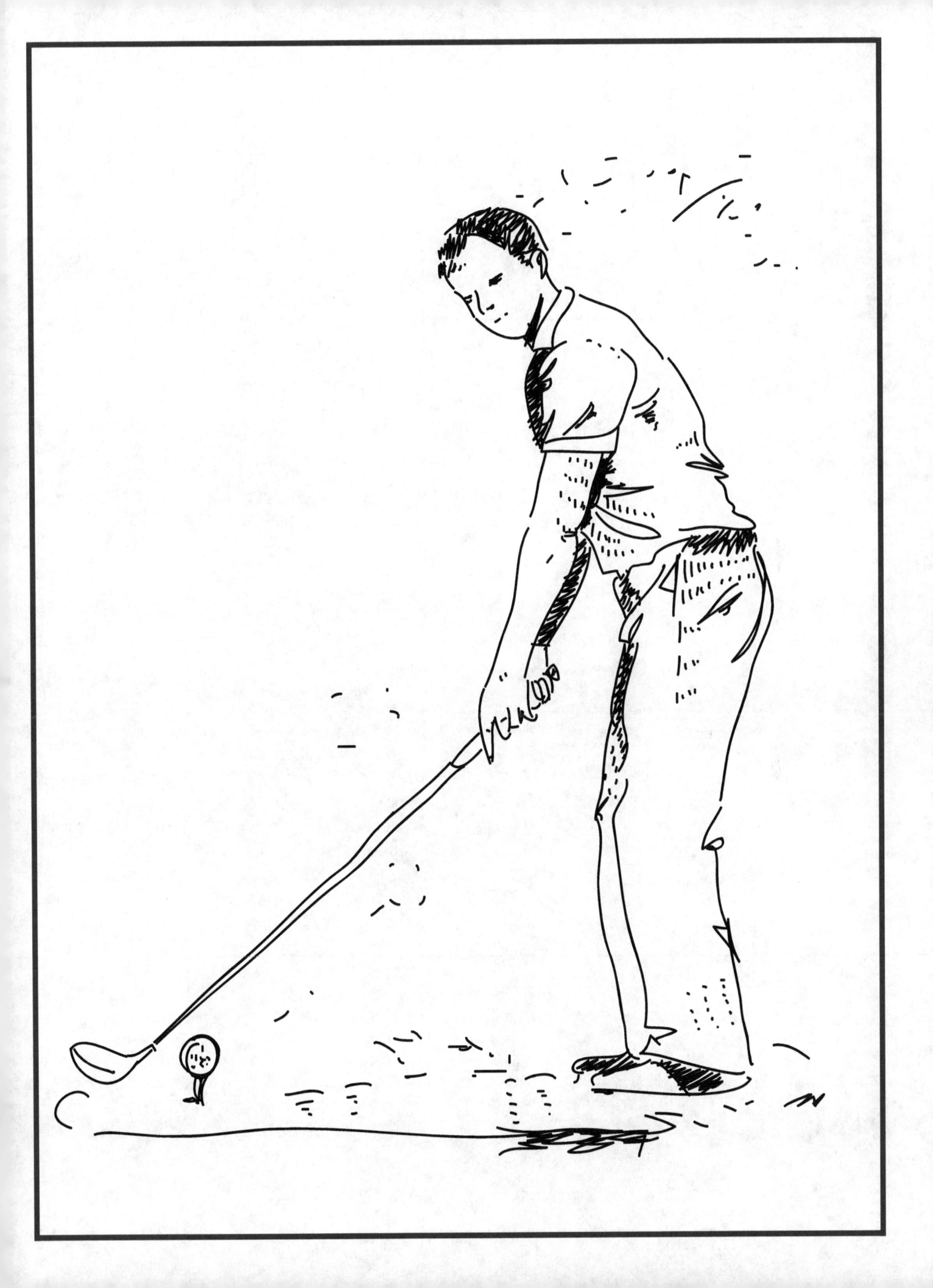

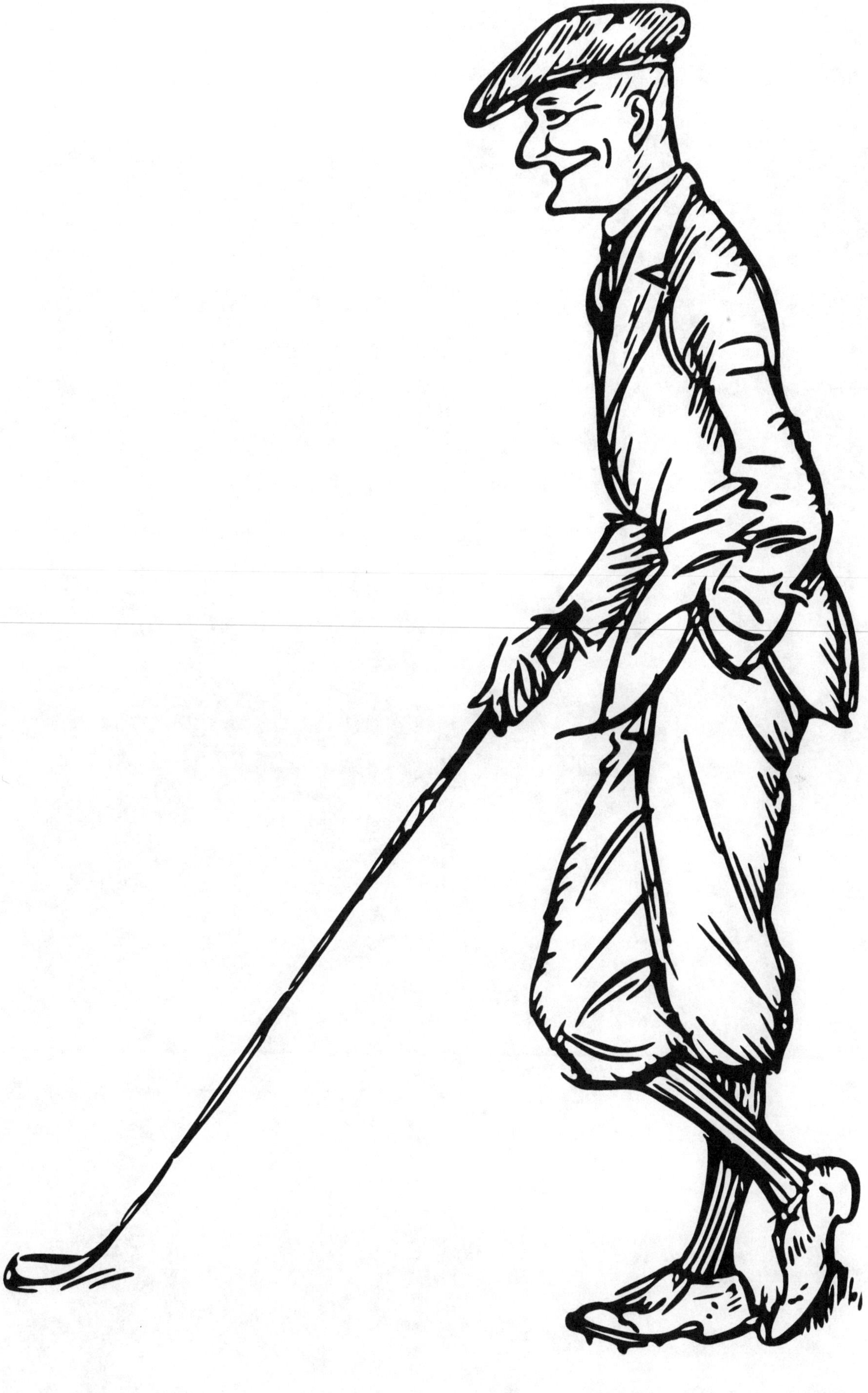

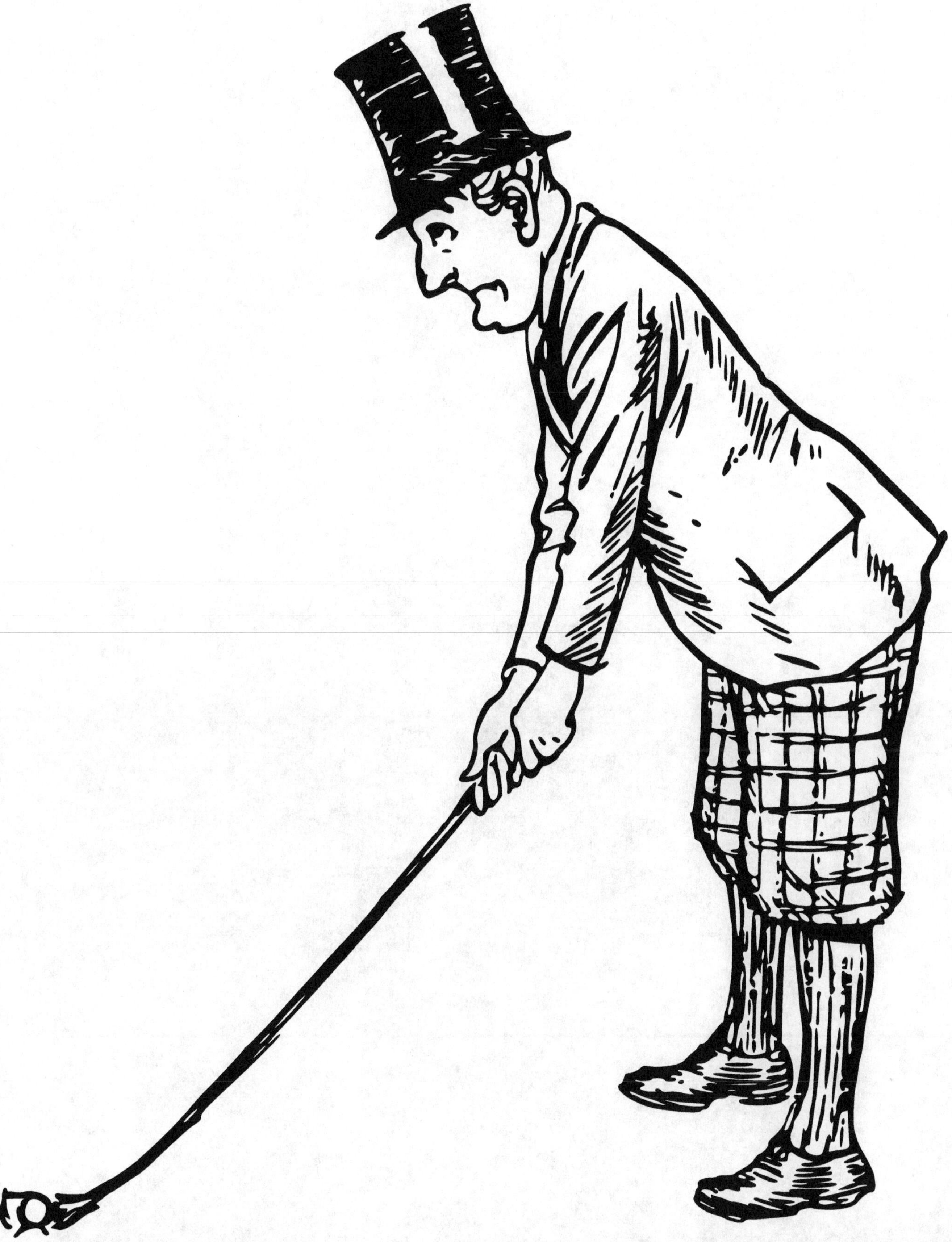

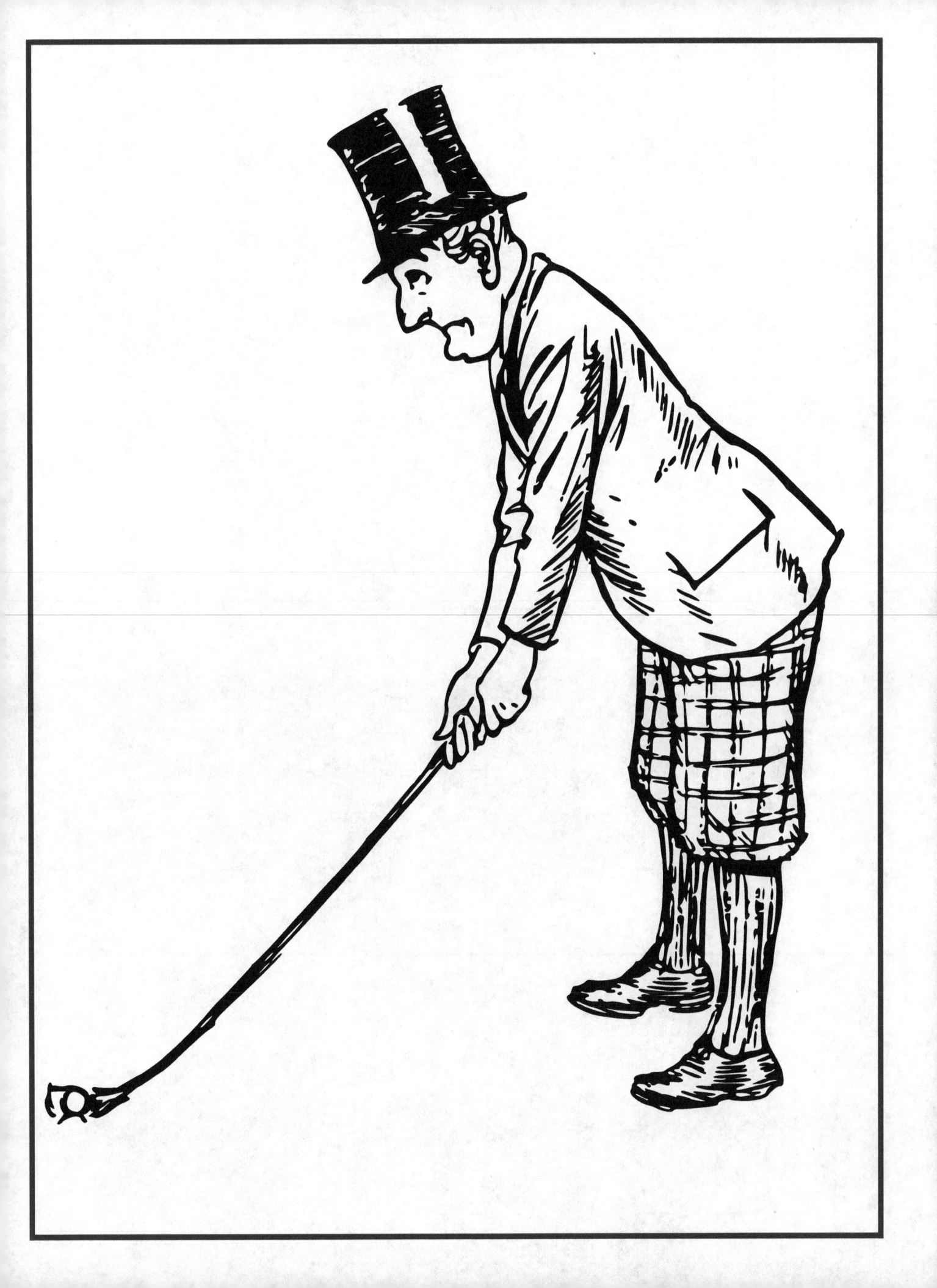

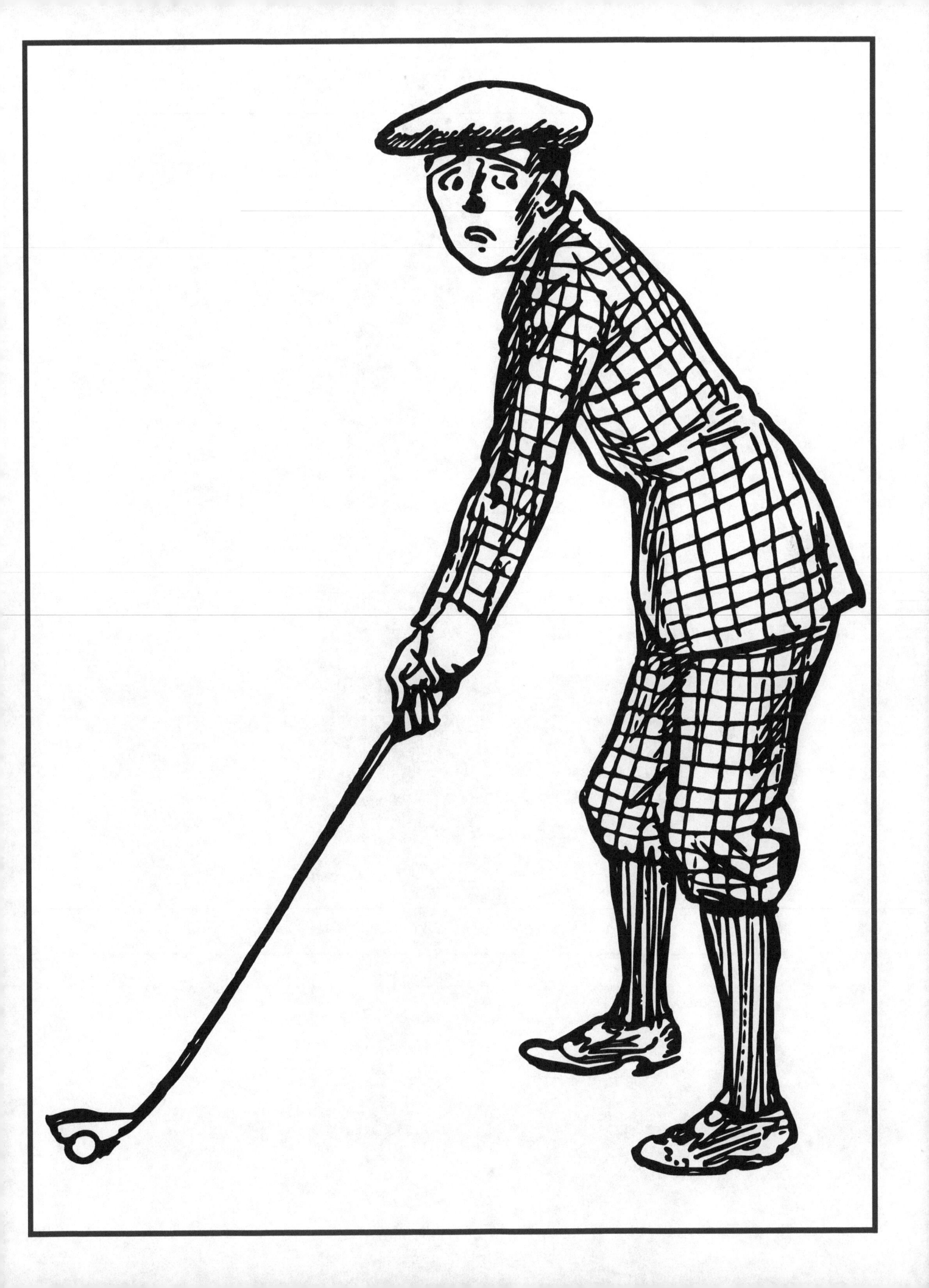

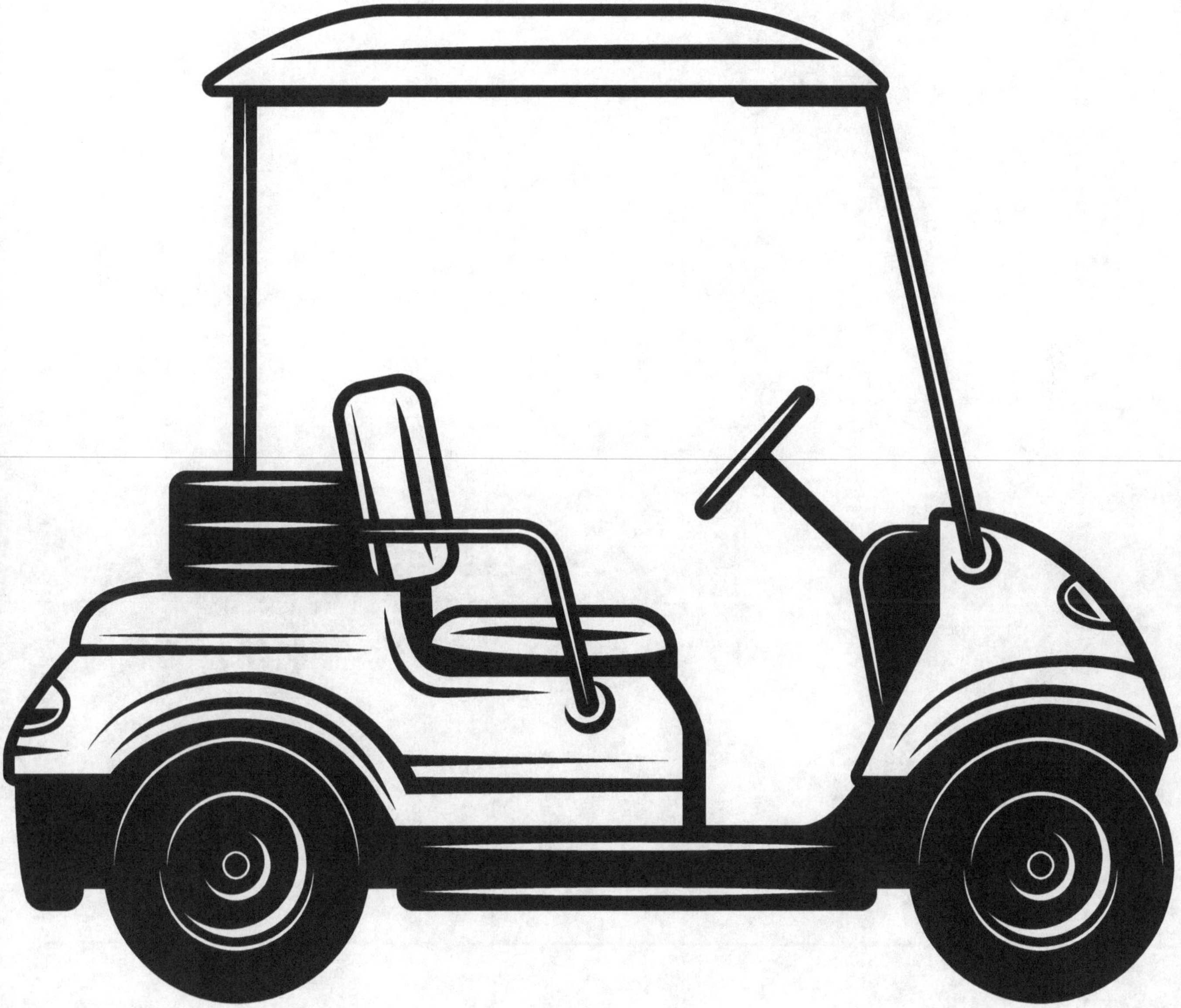

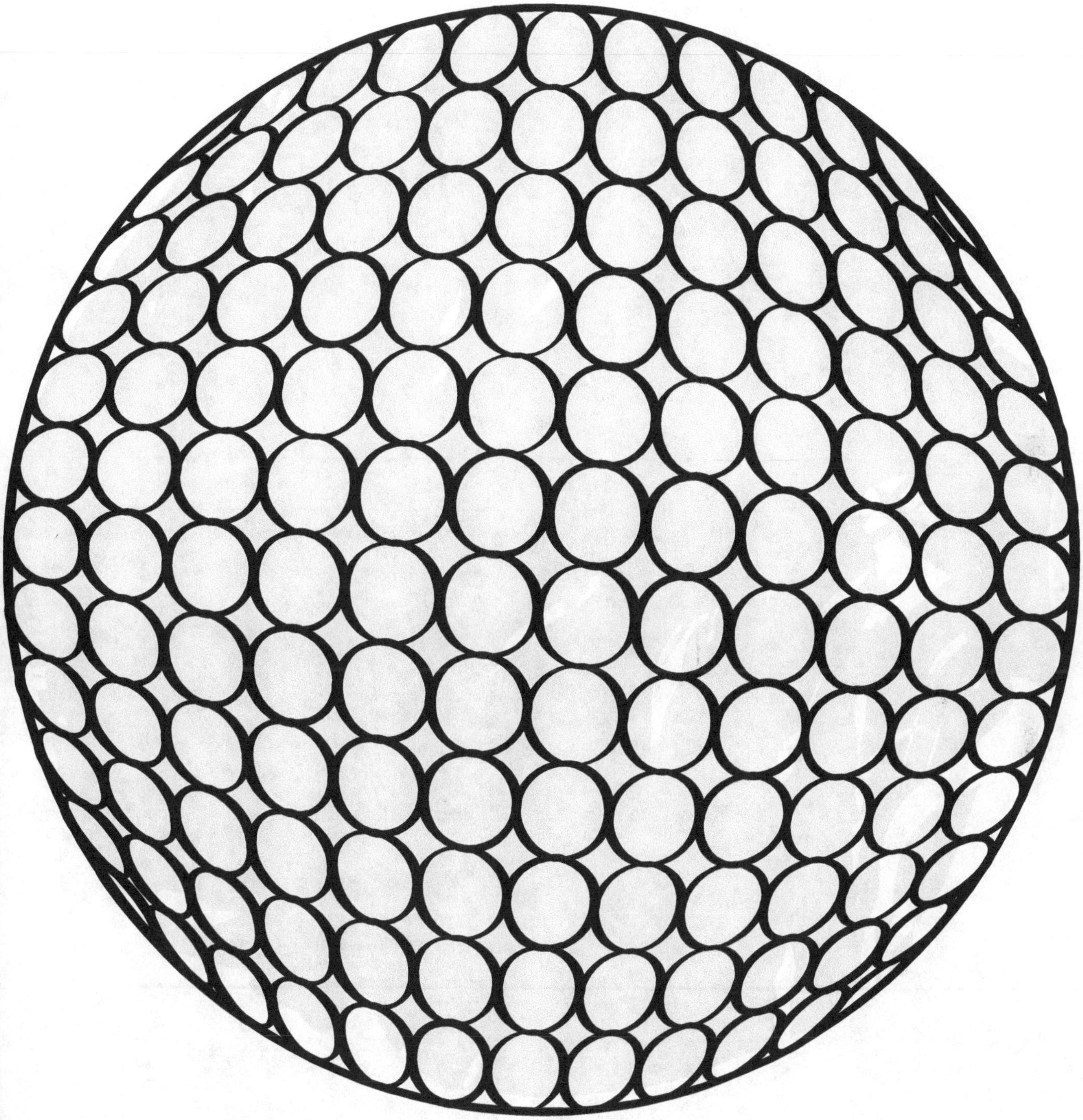

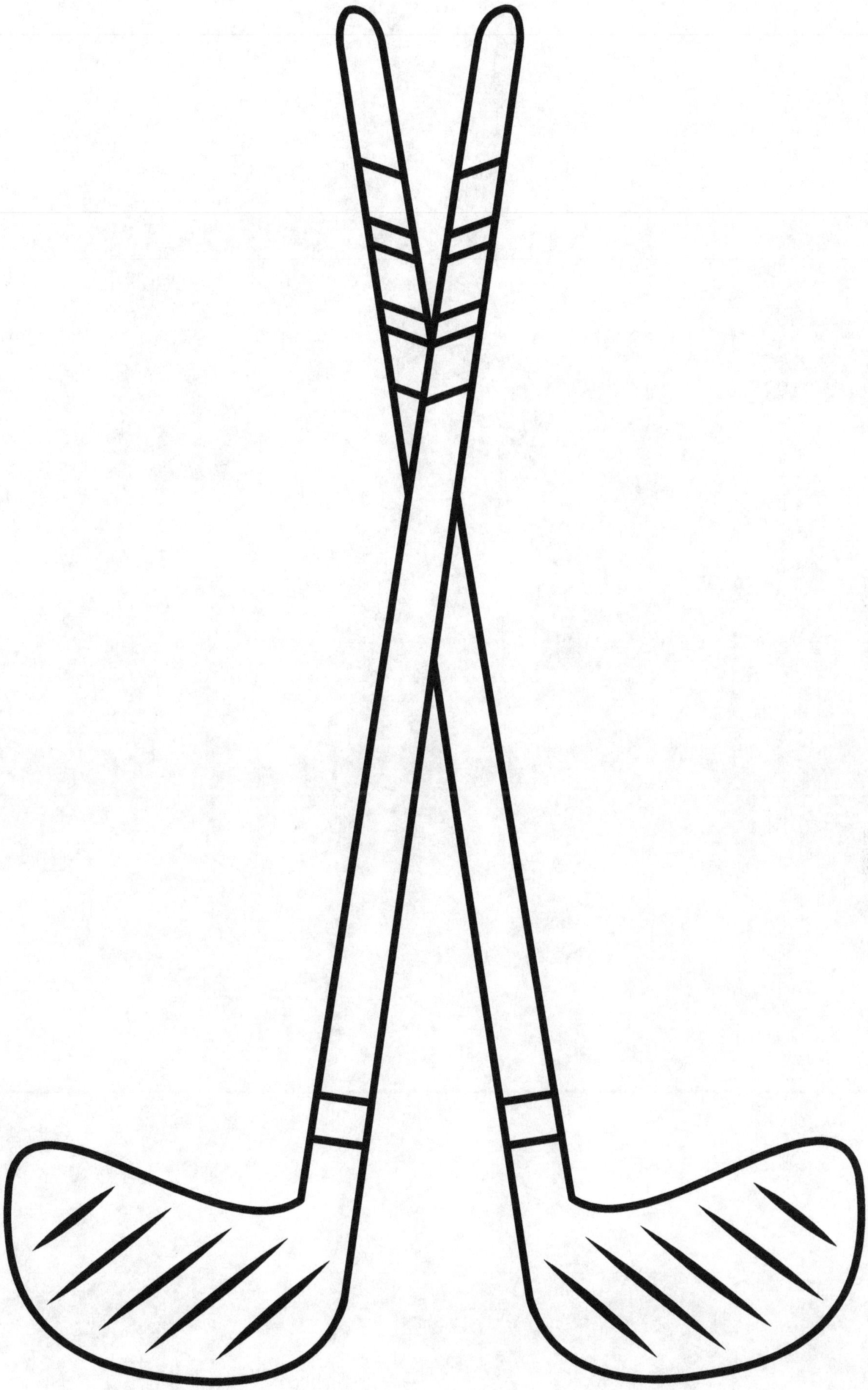

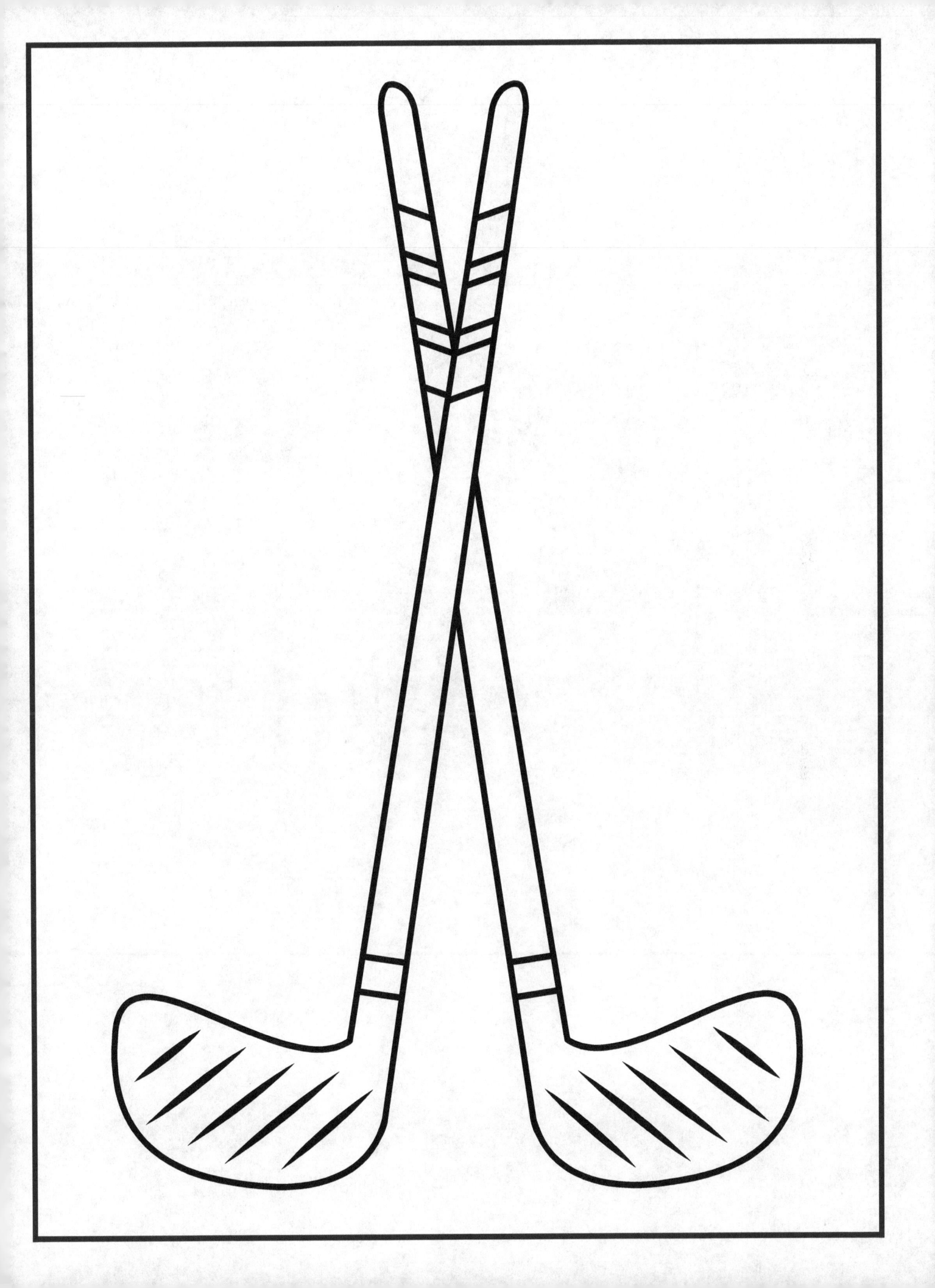

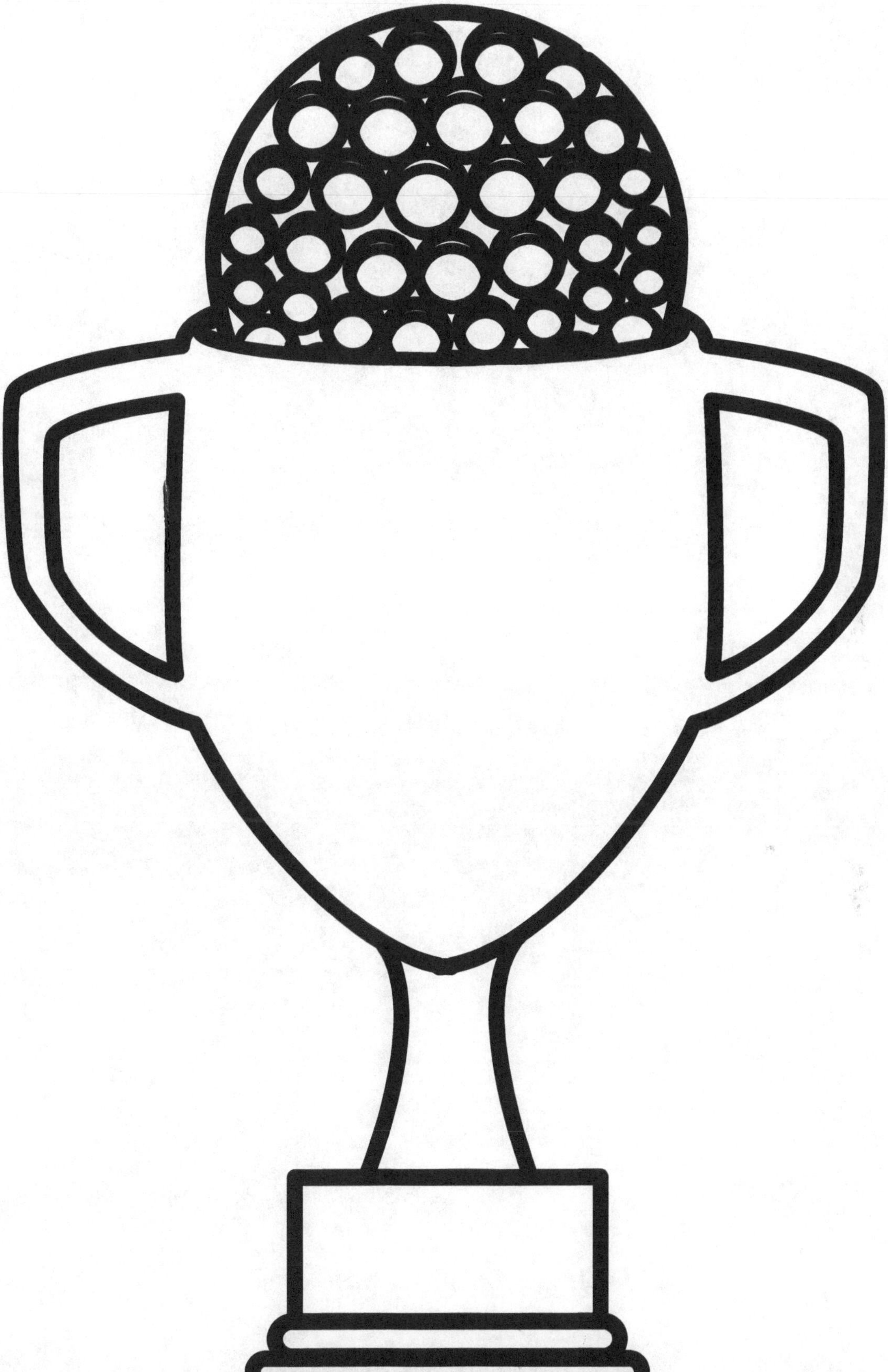

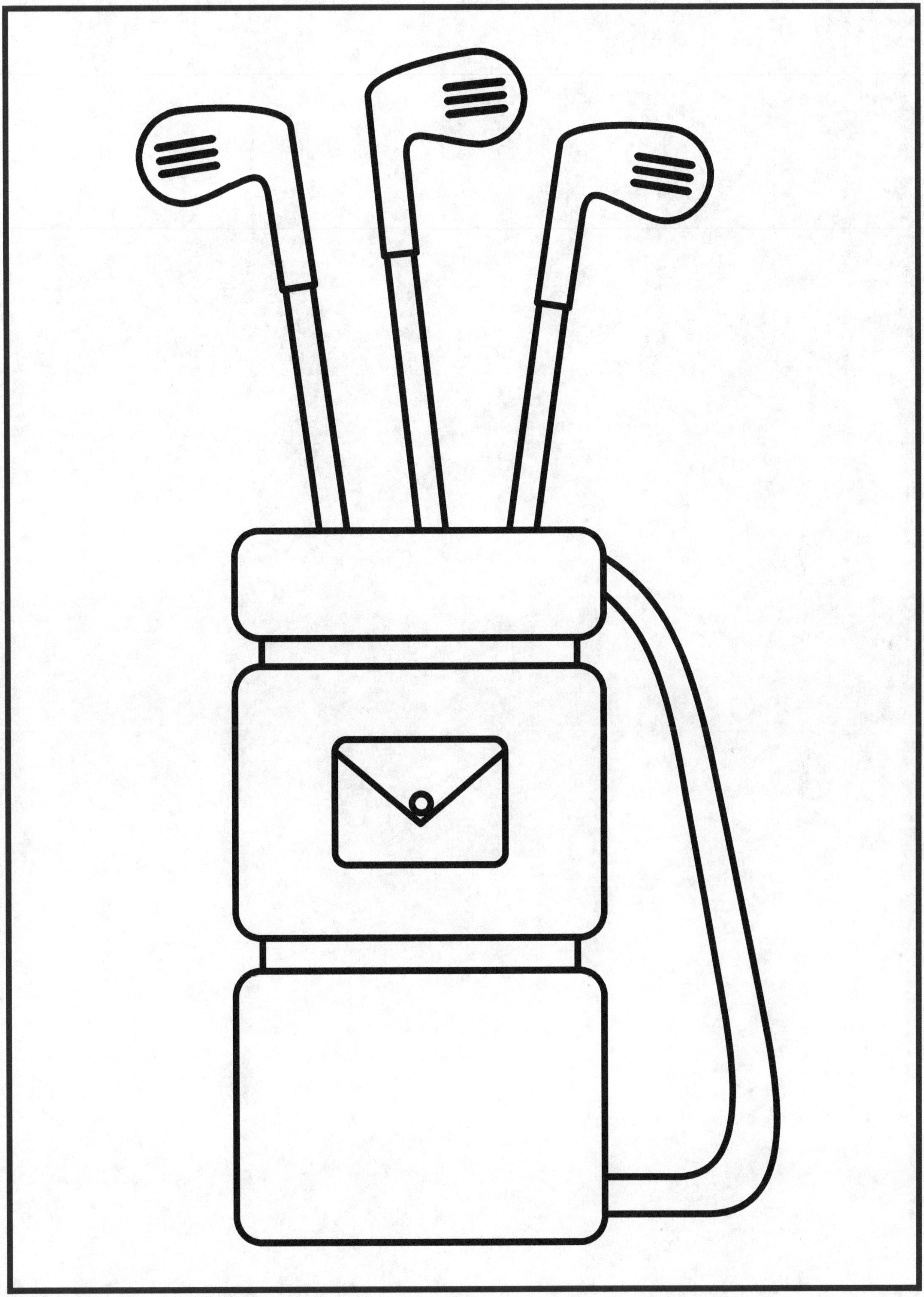

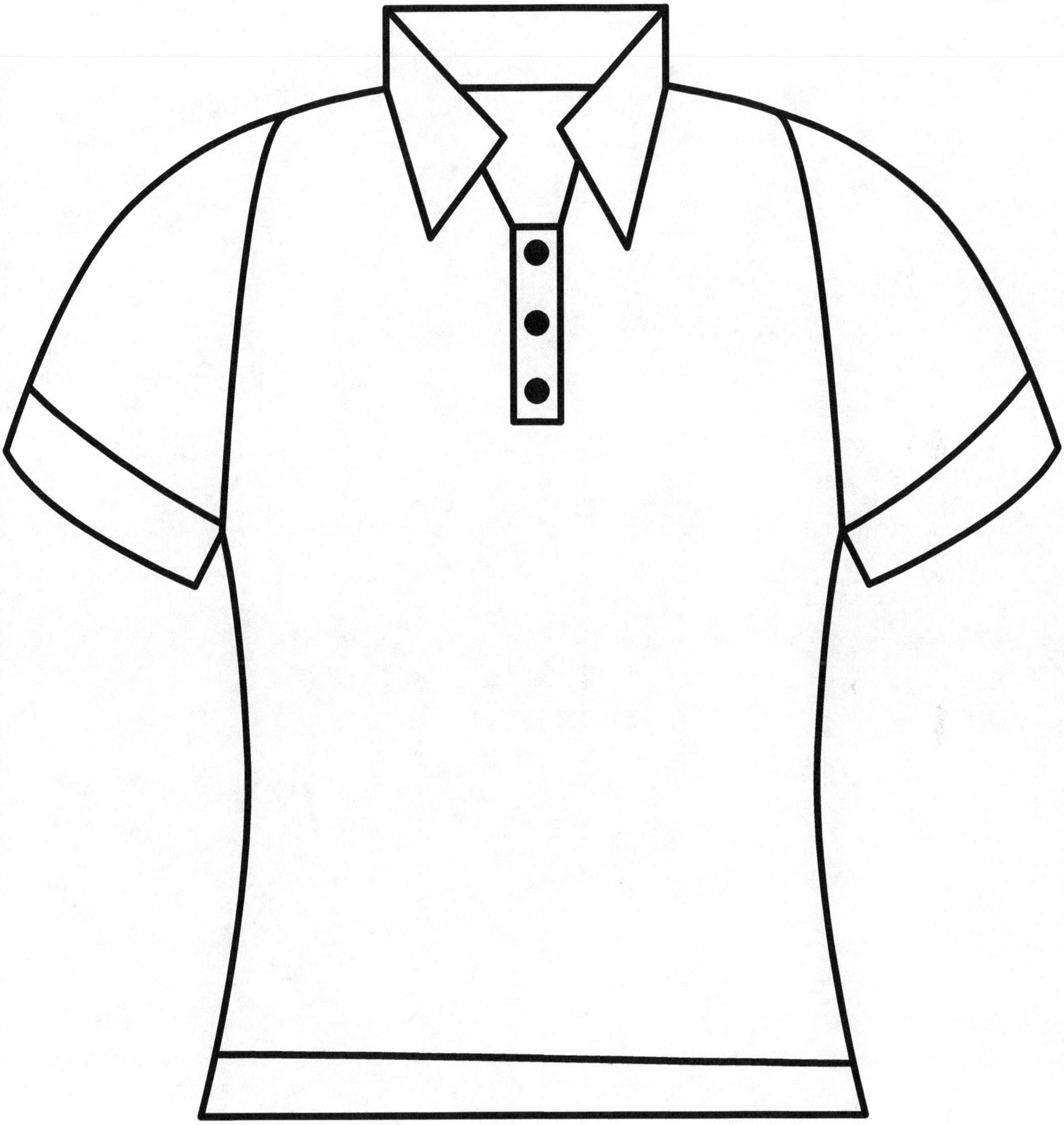

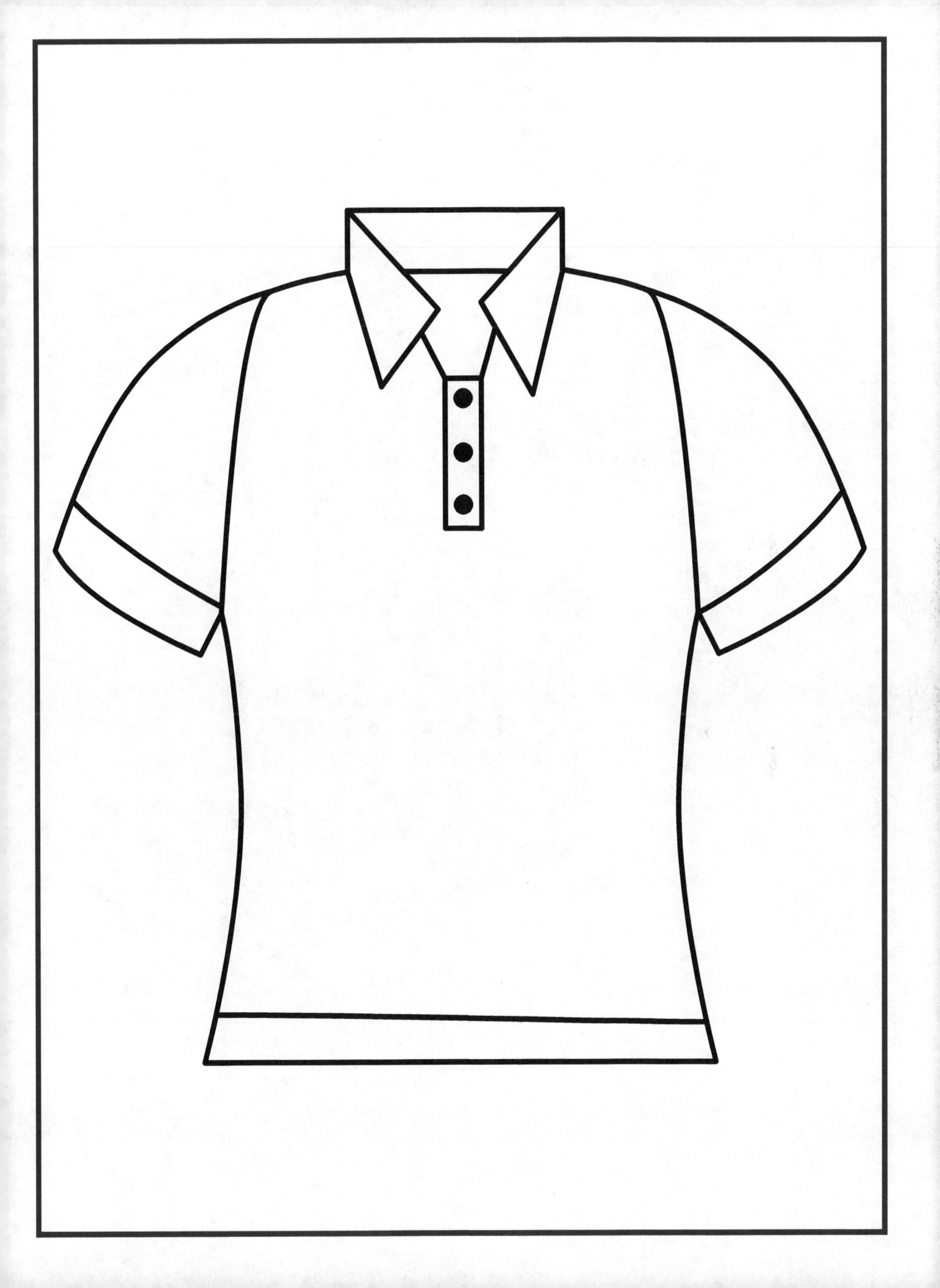

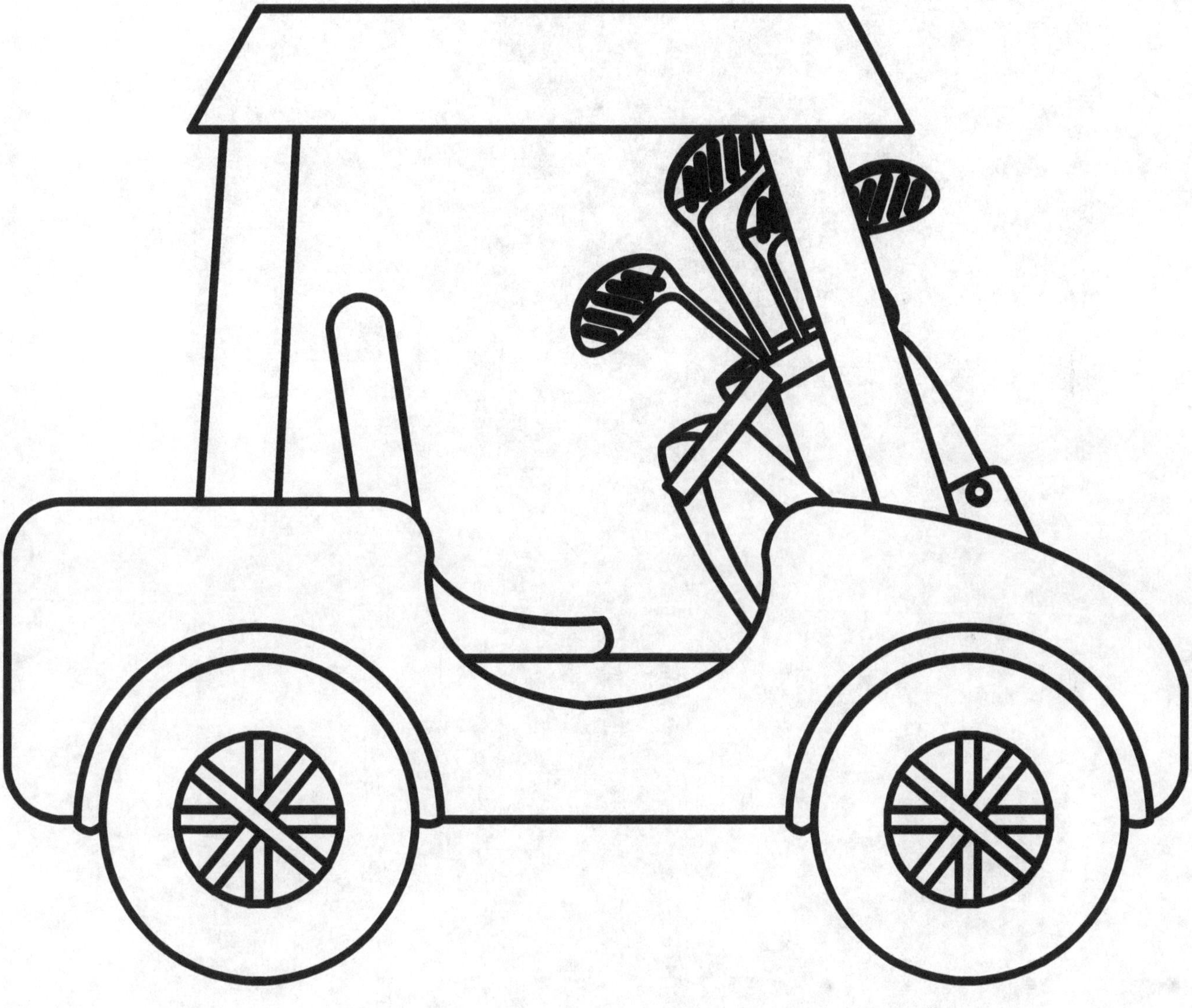

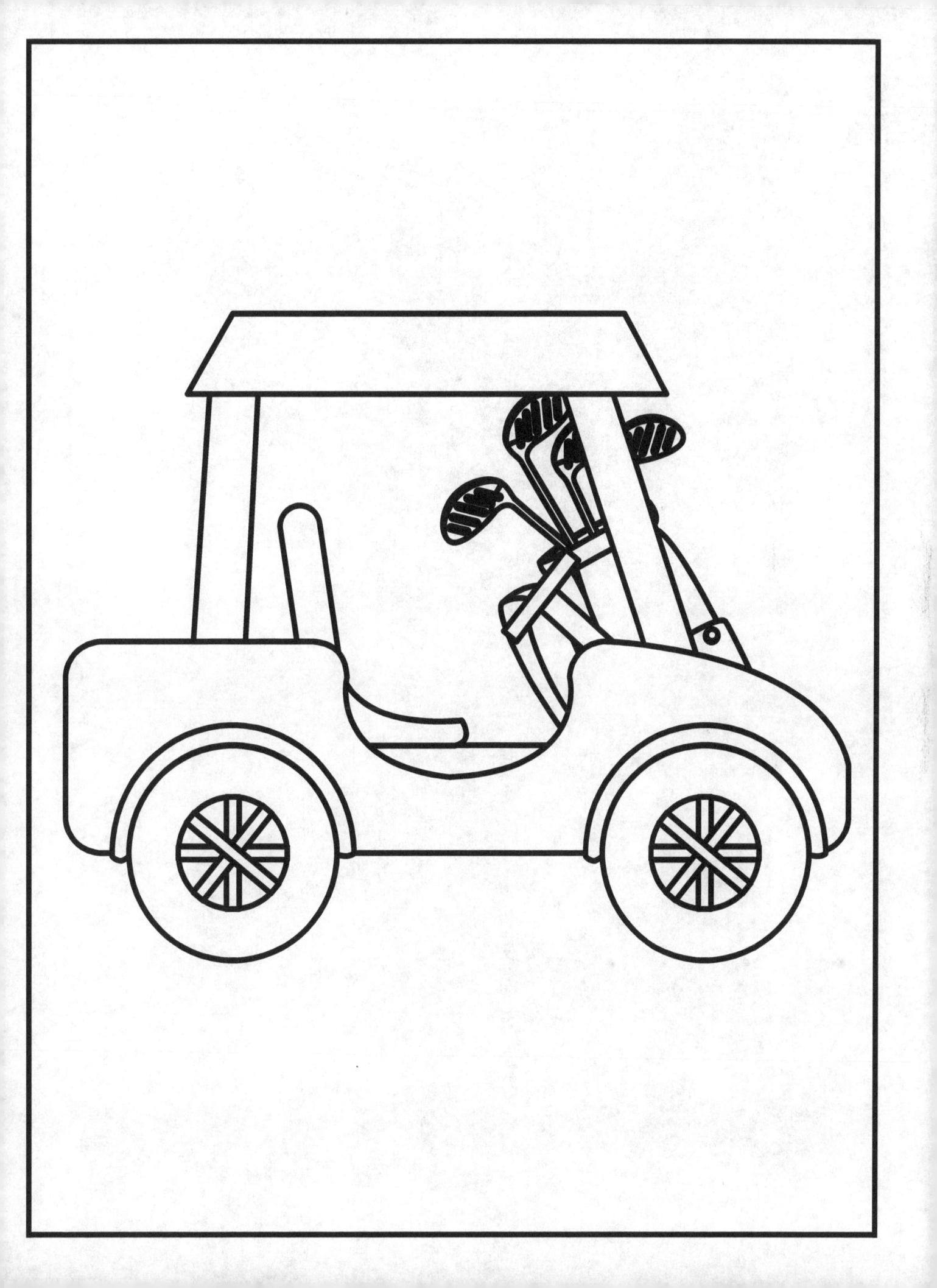

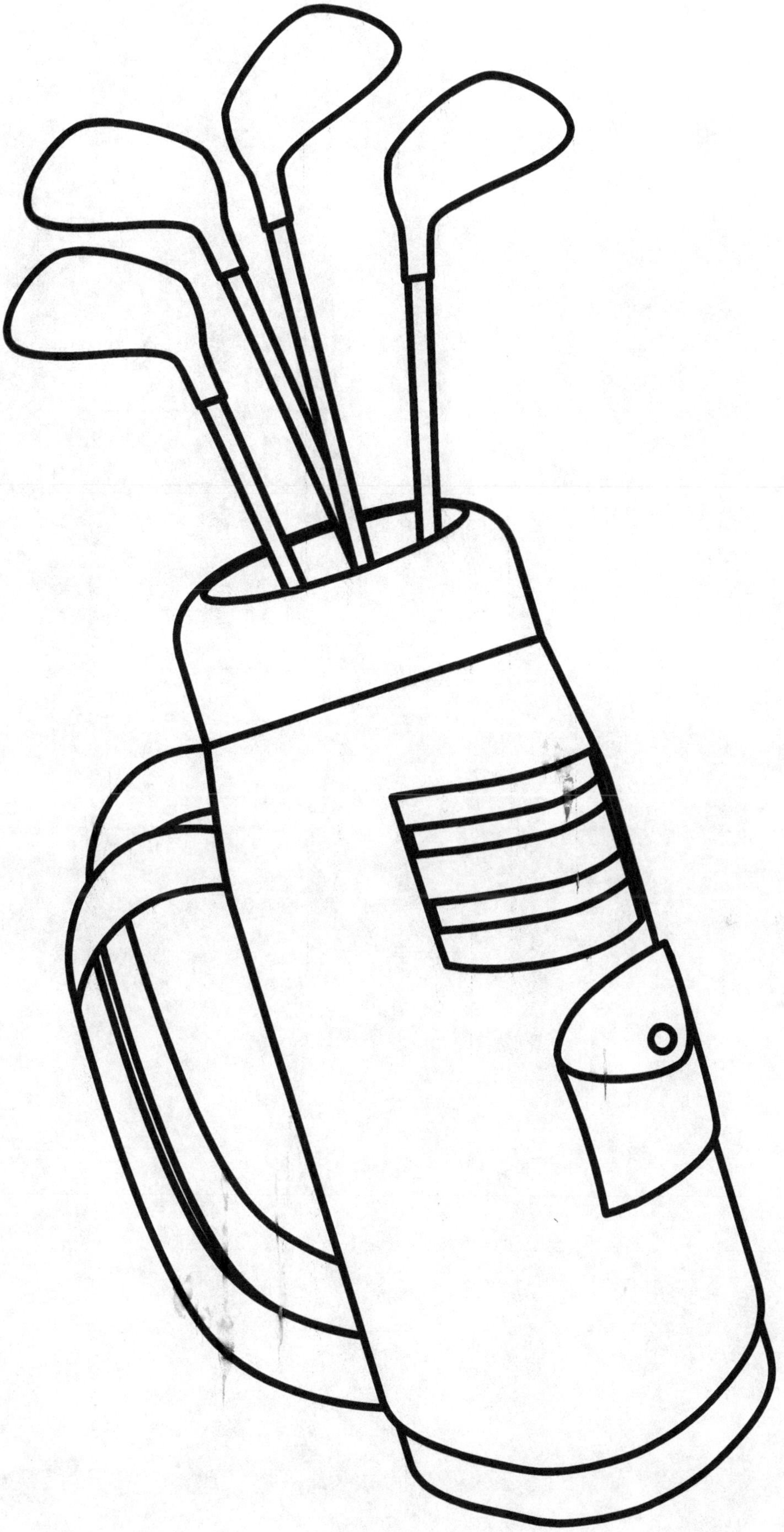

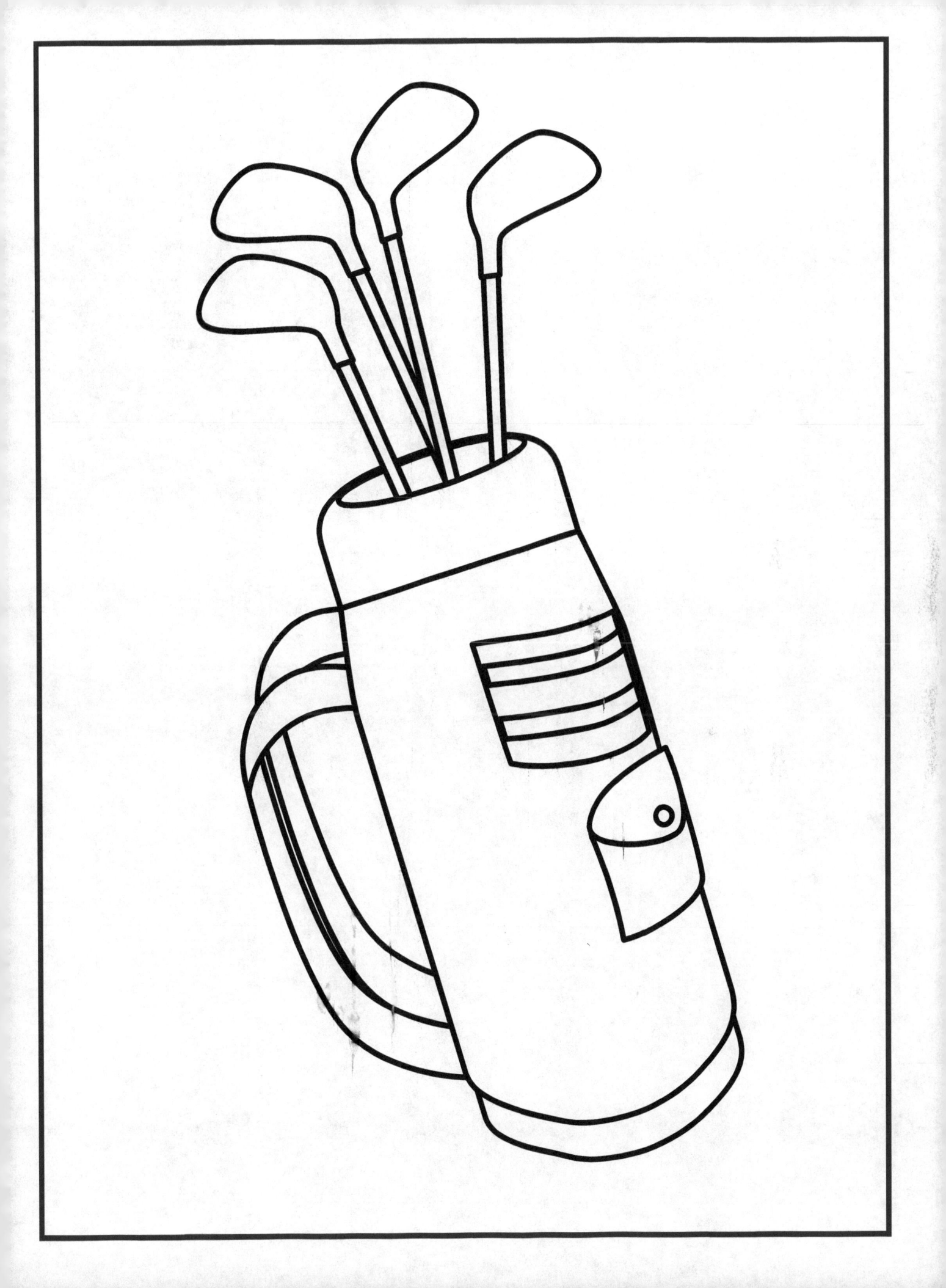

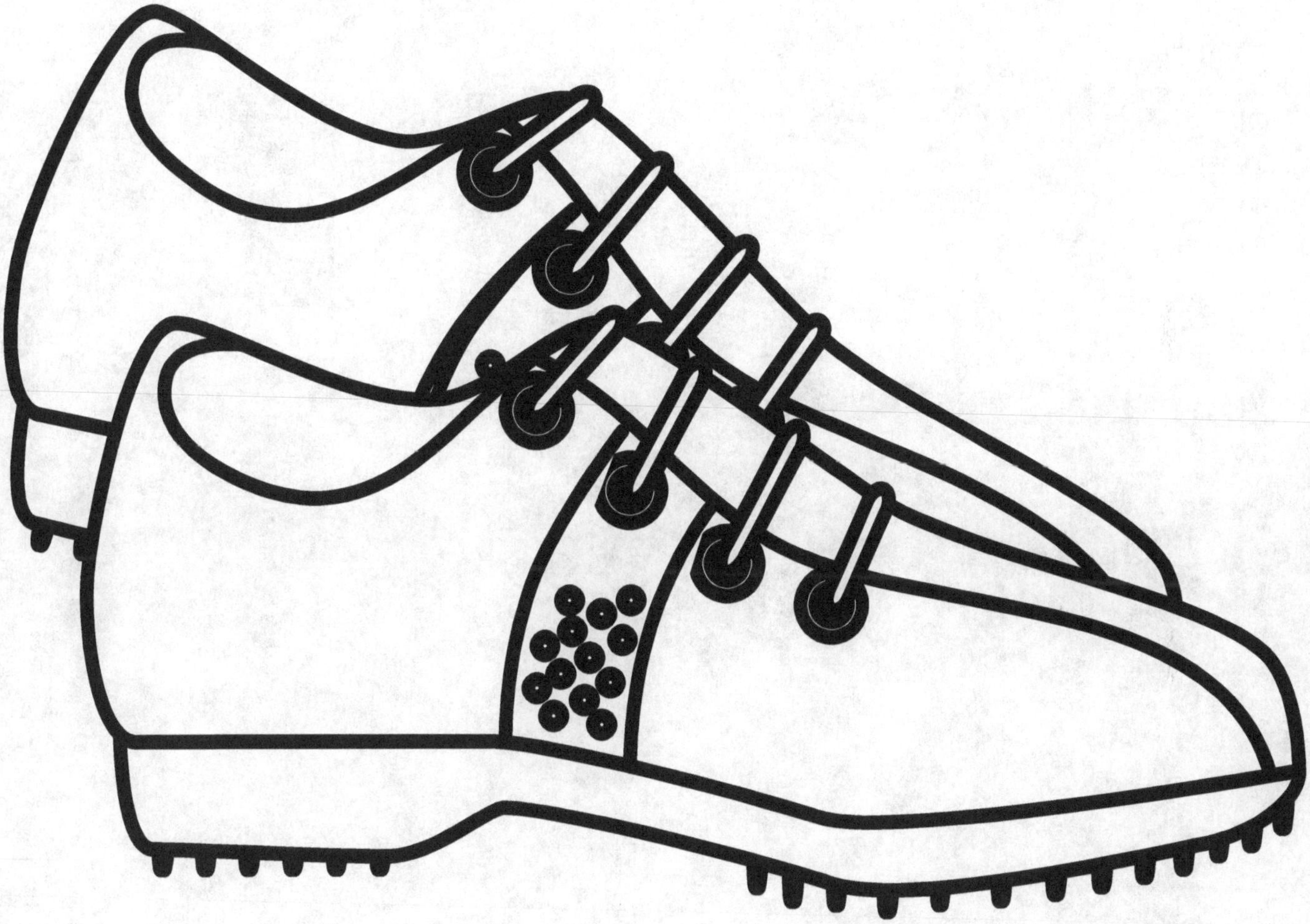

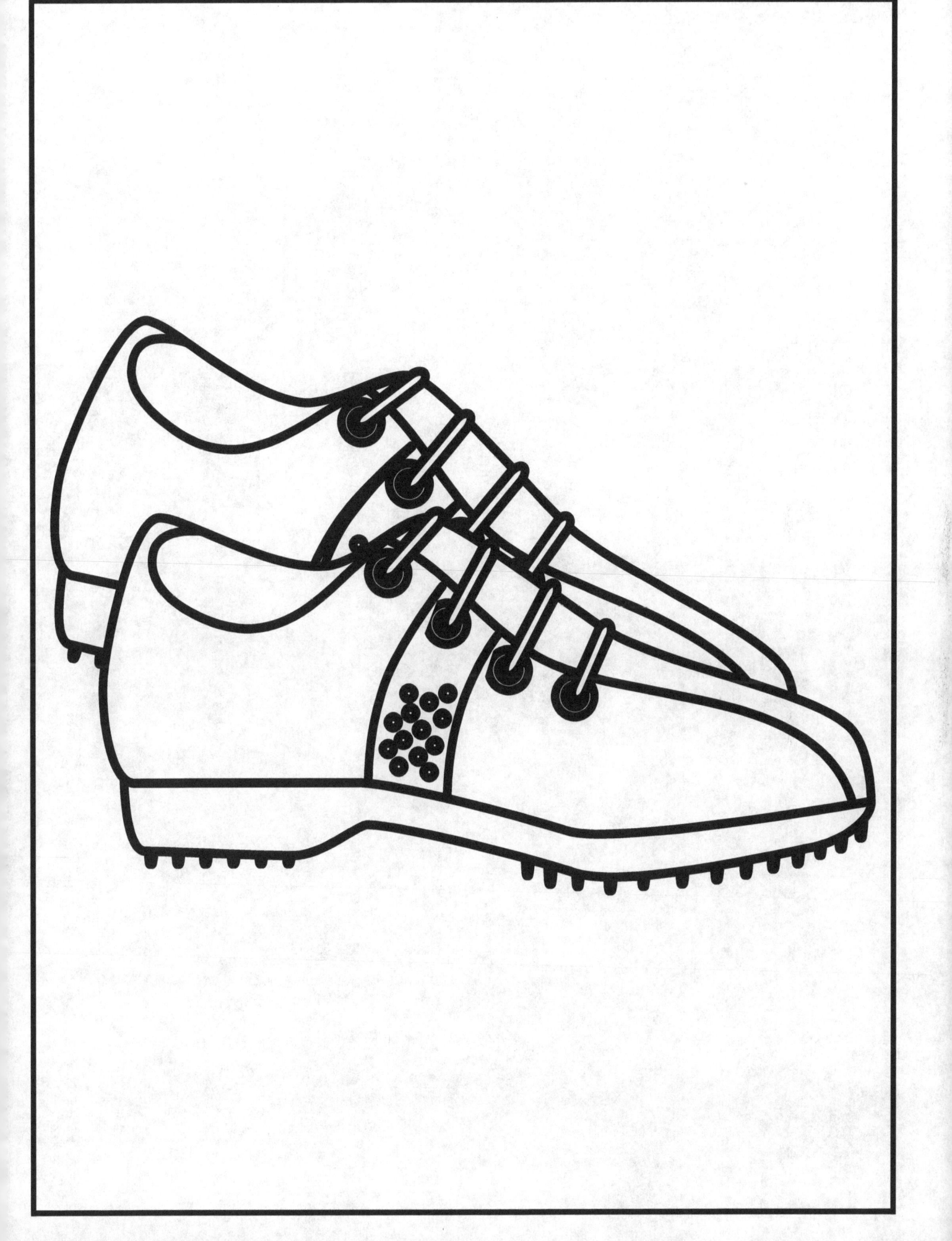

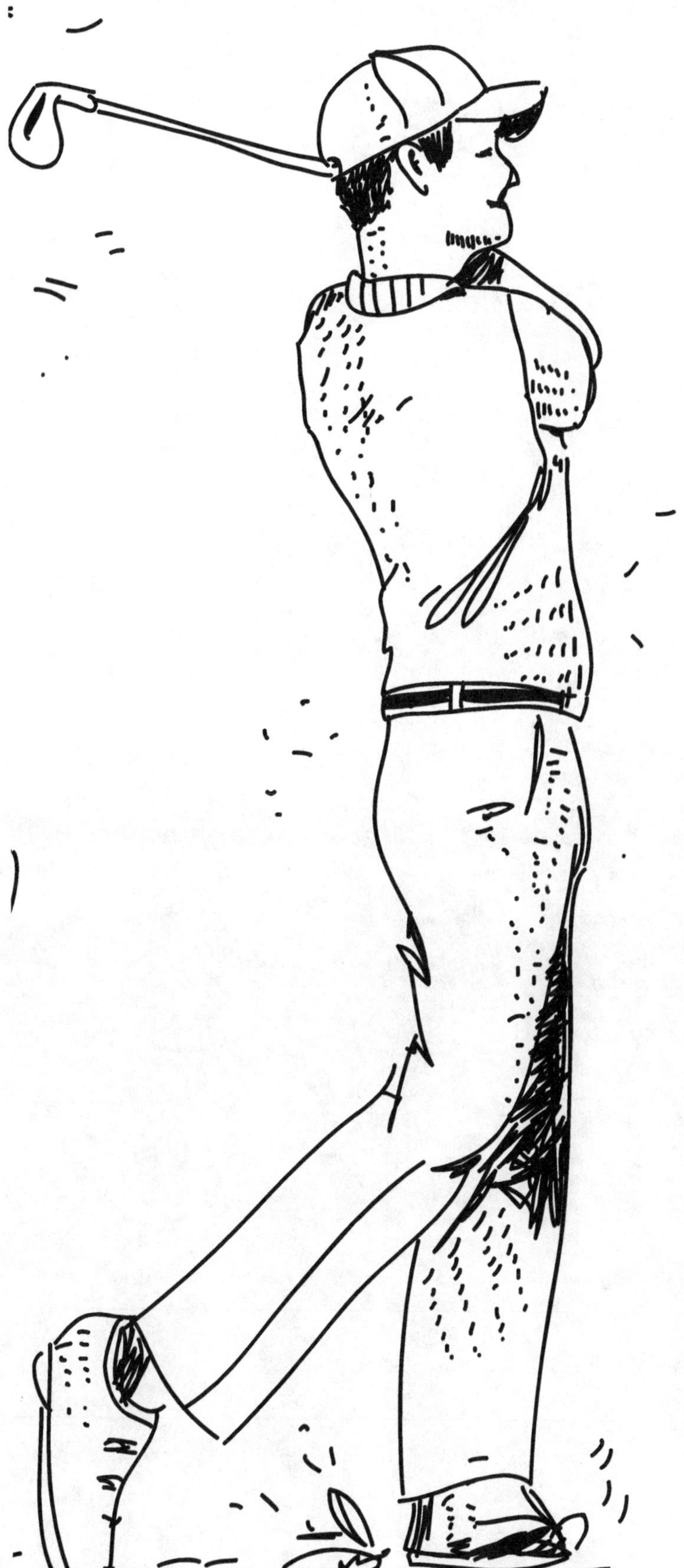

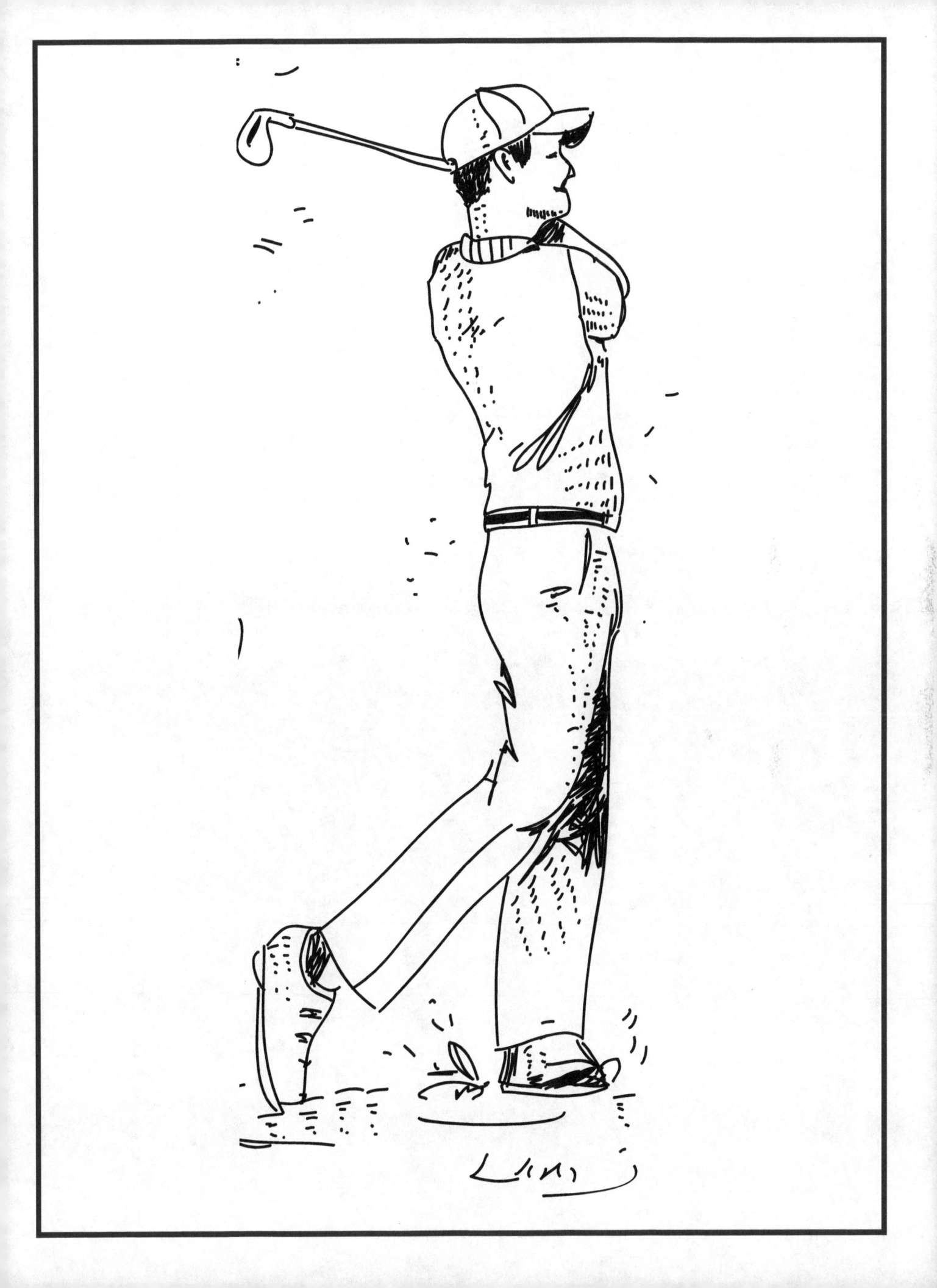

GOLF

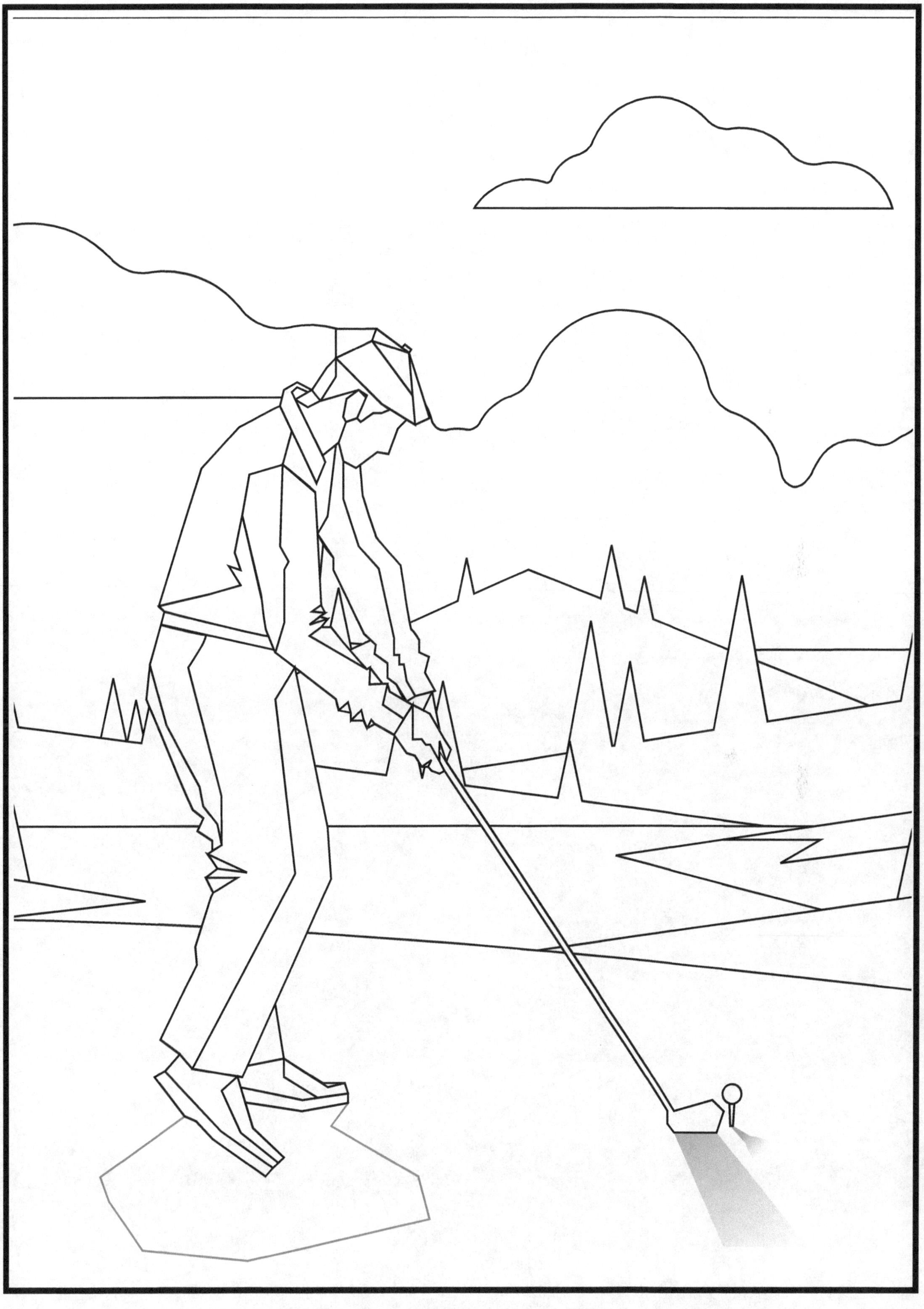

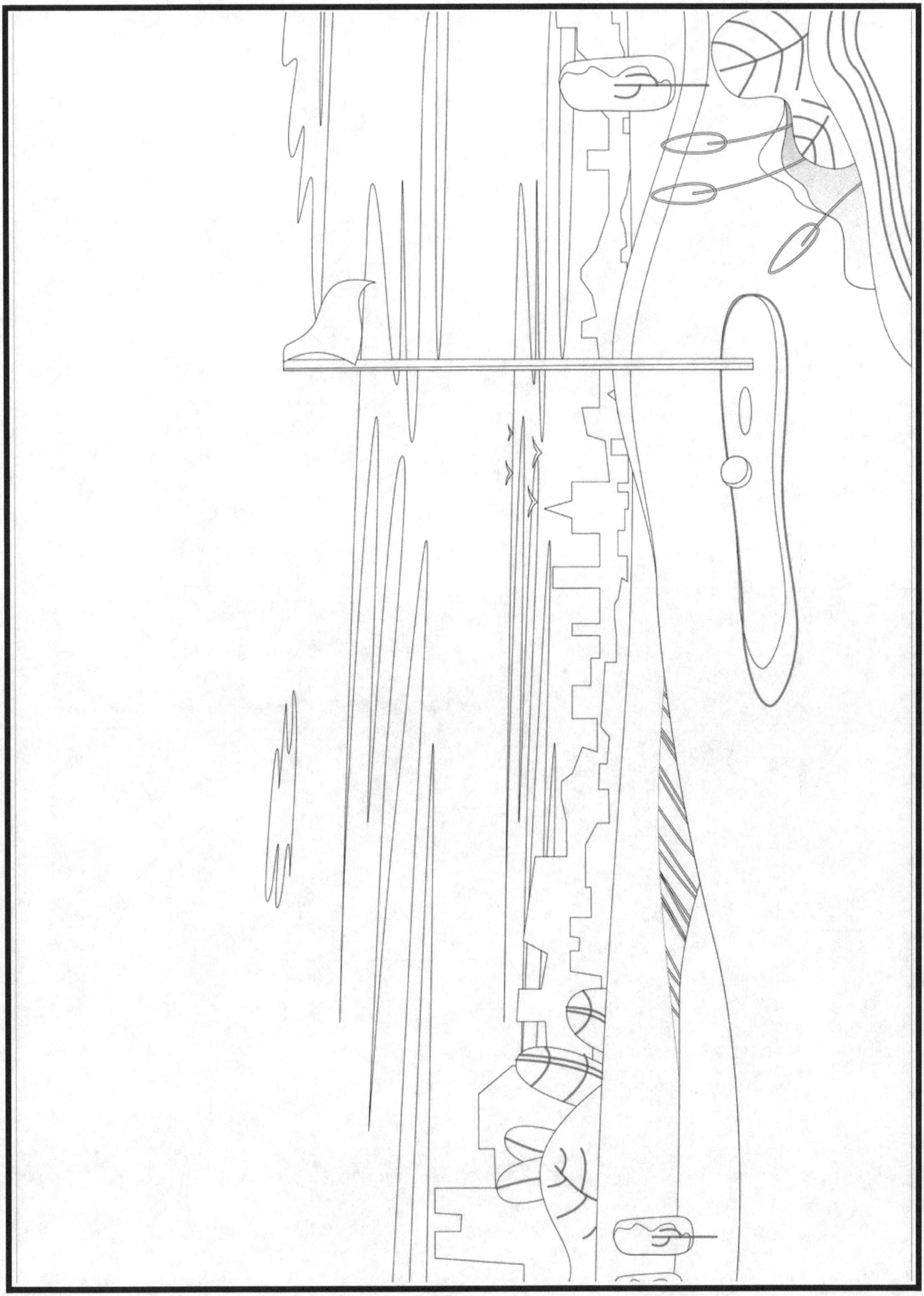

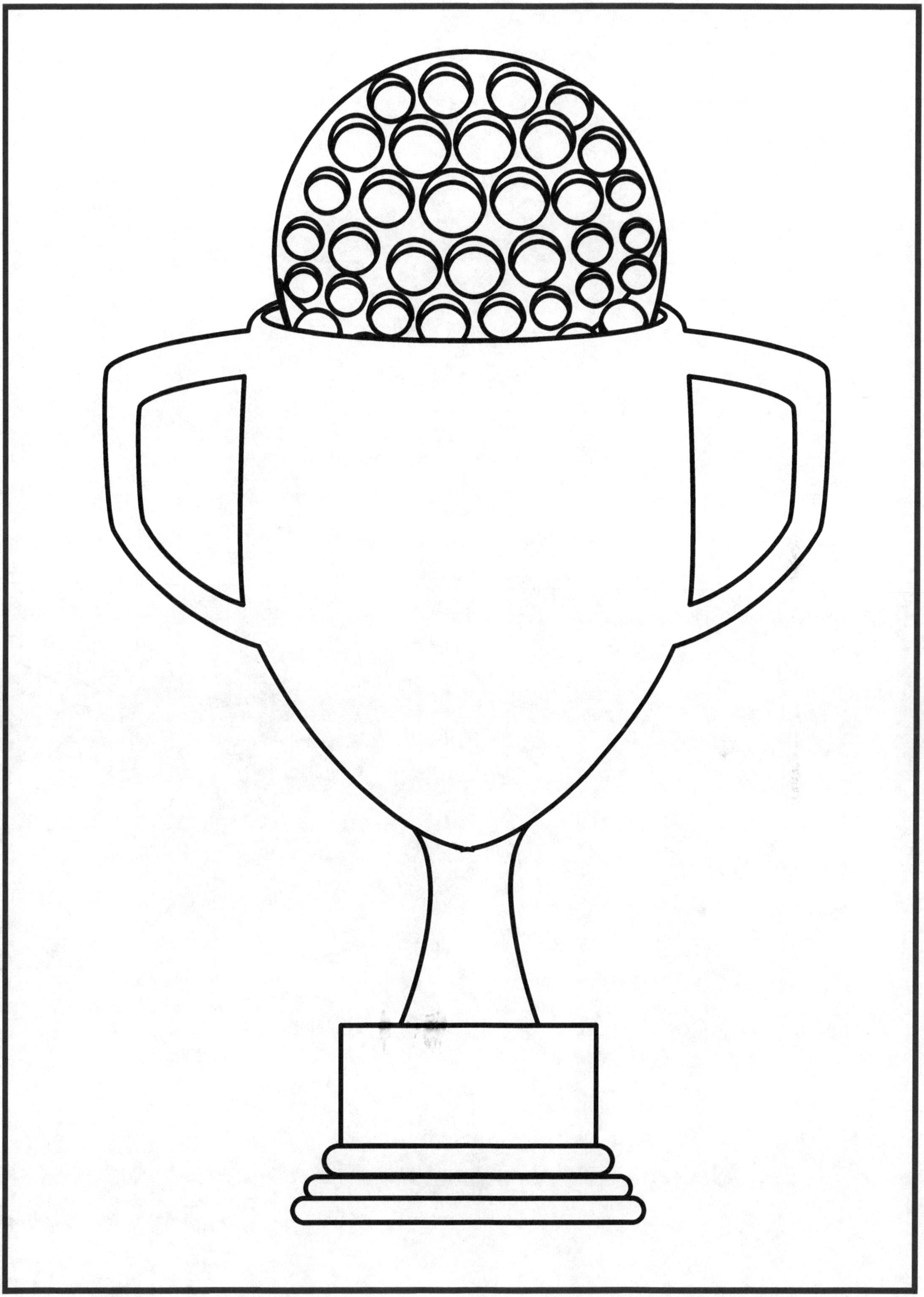

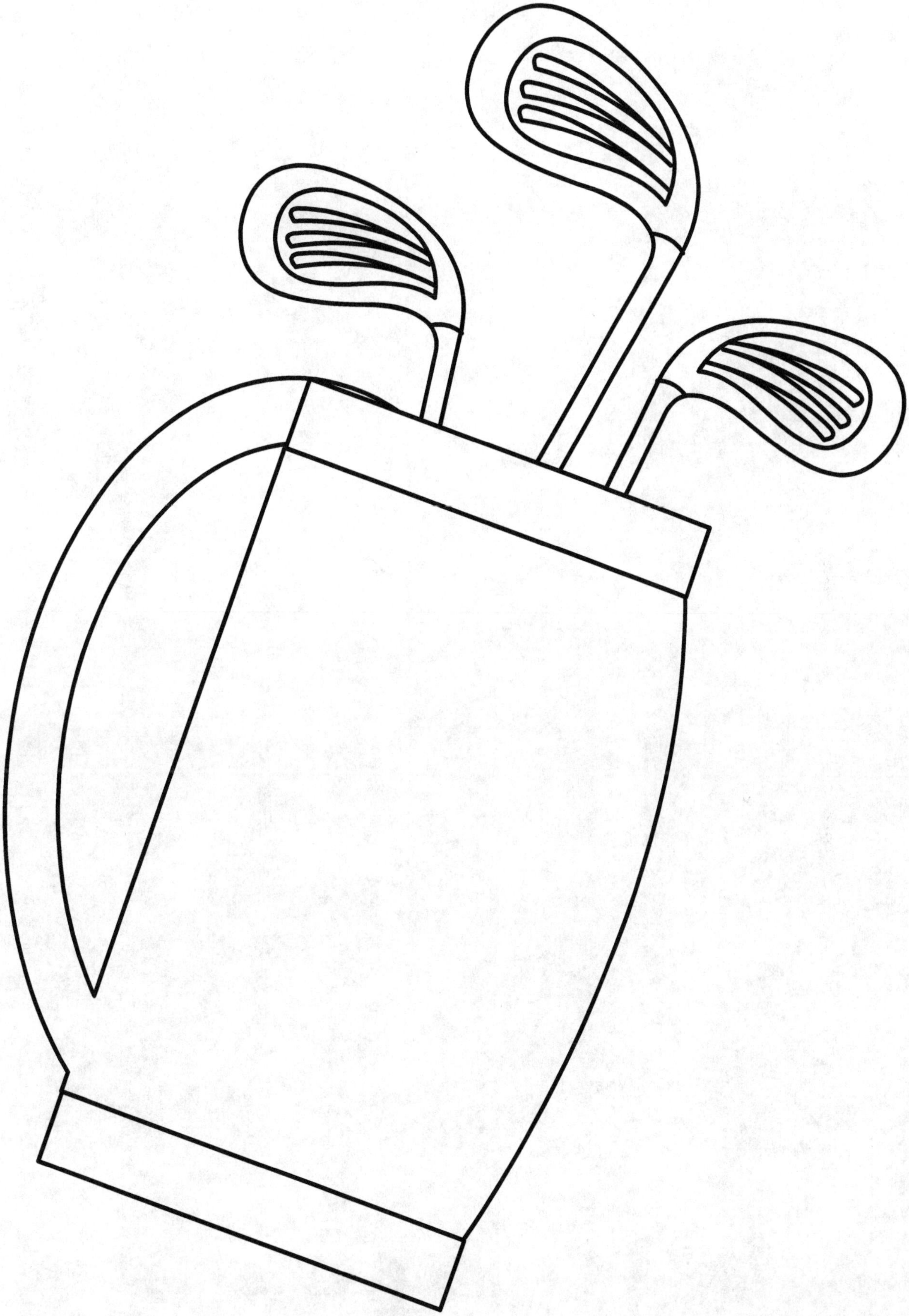

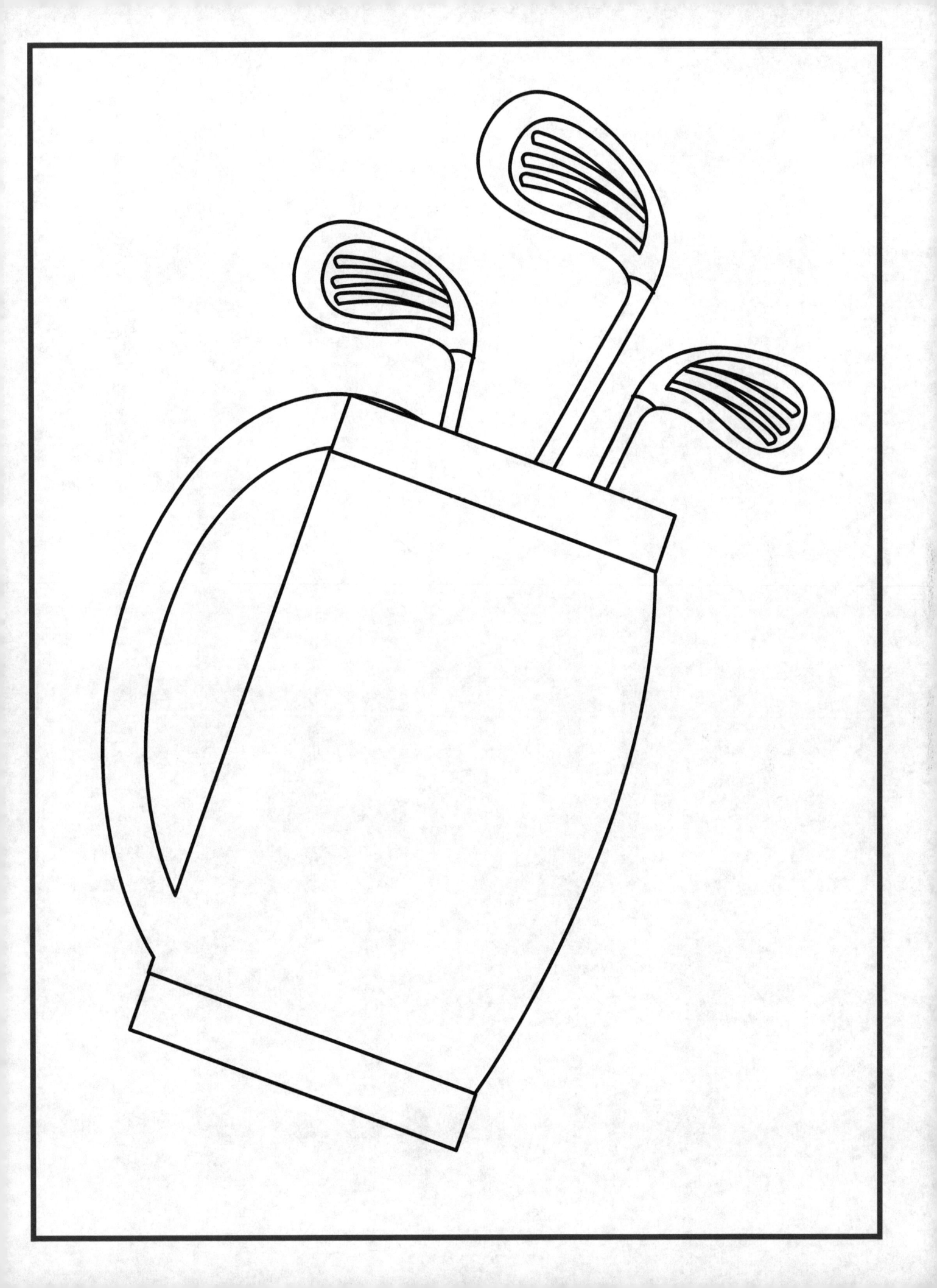

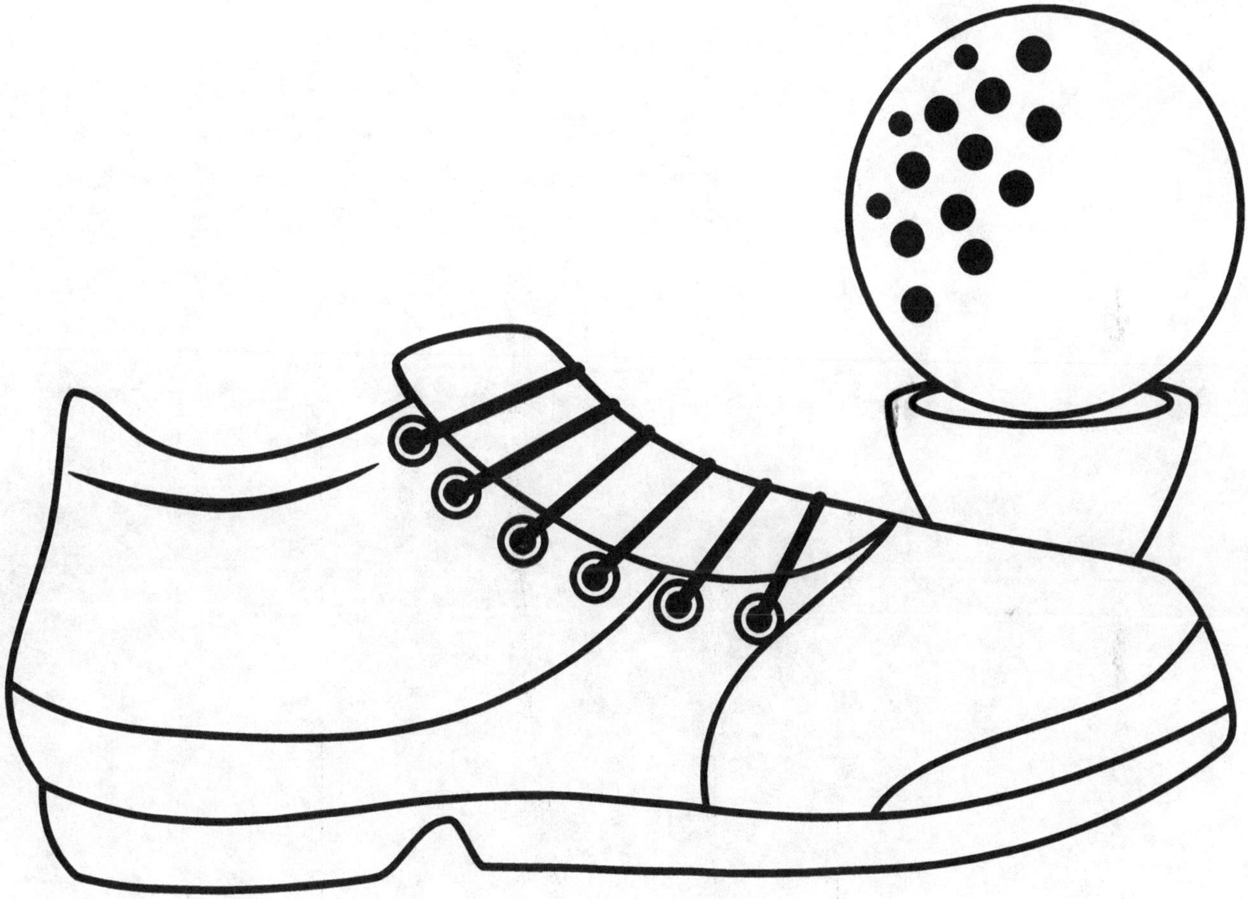

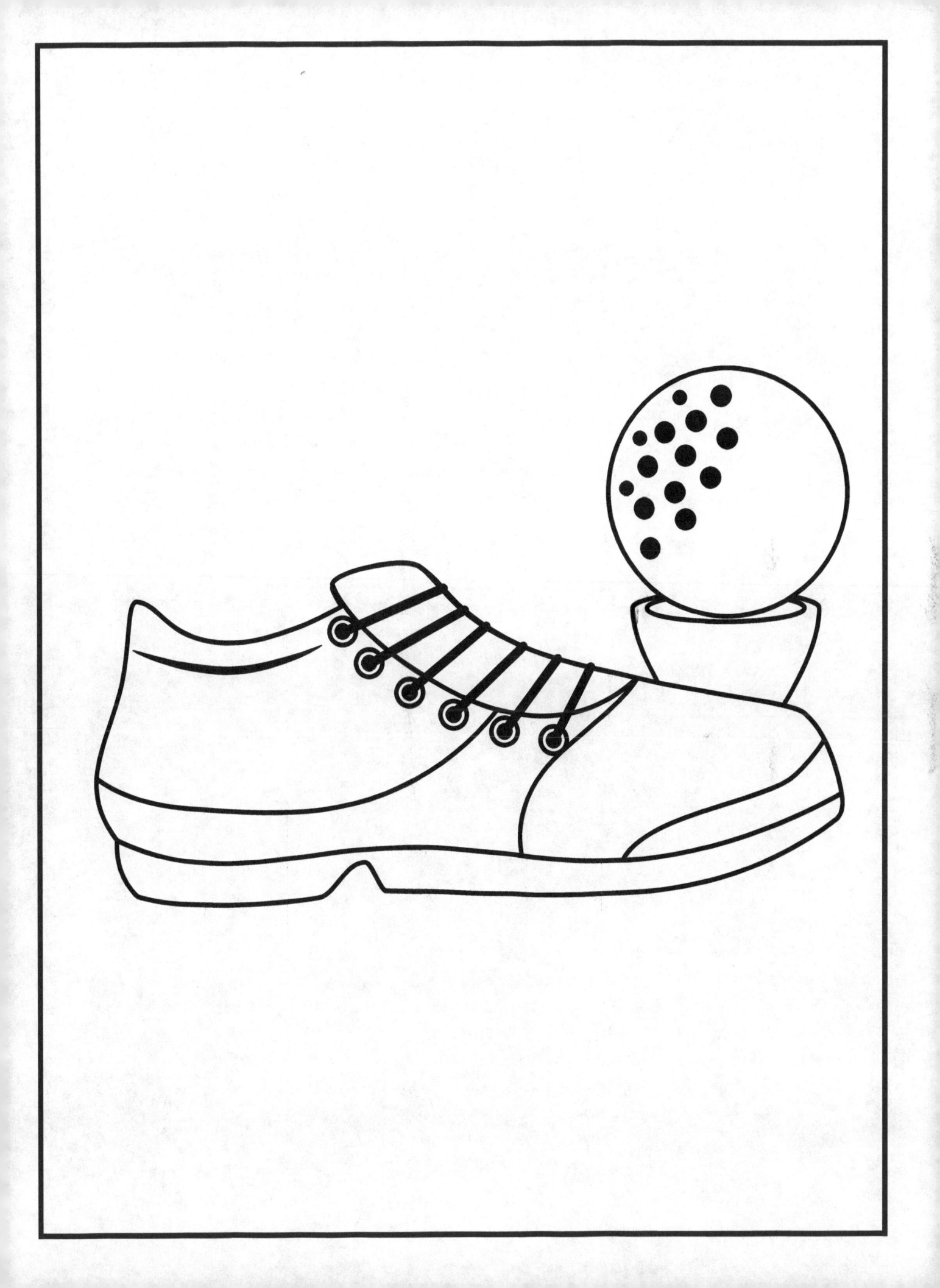

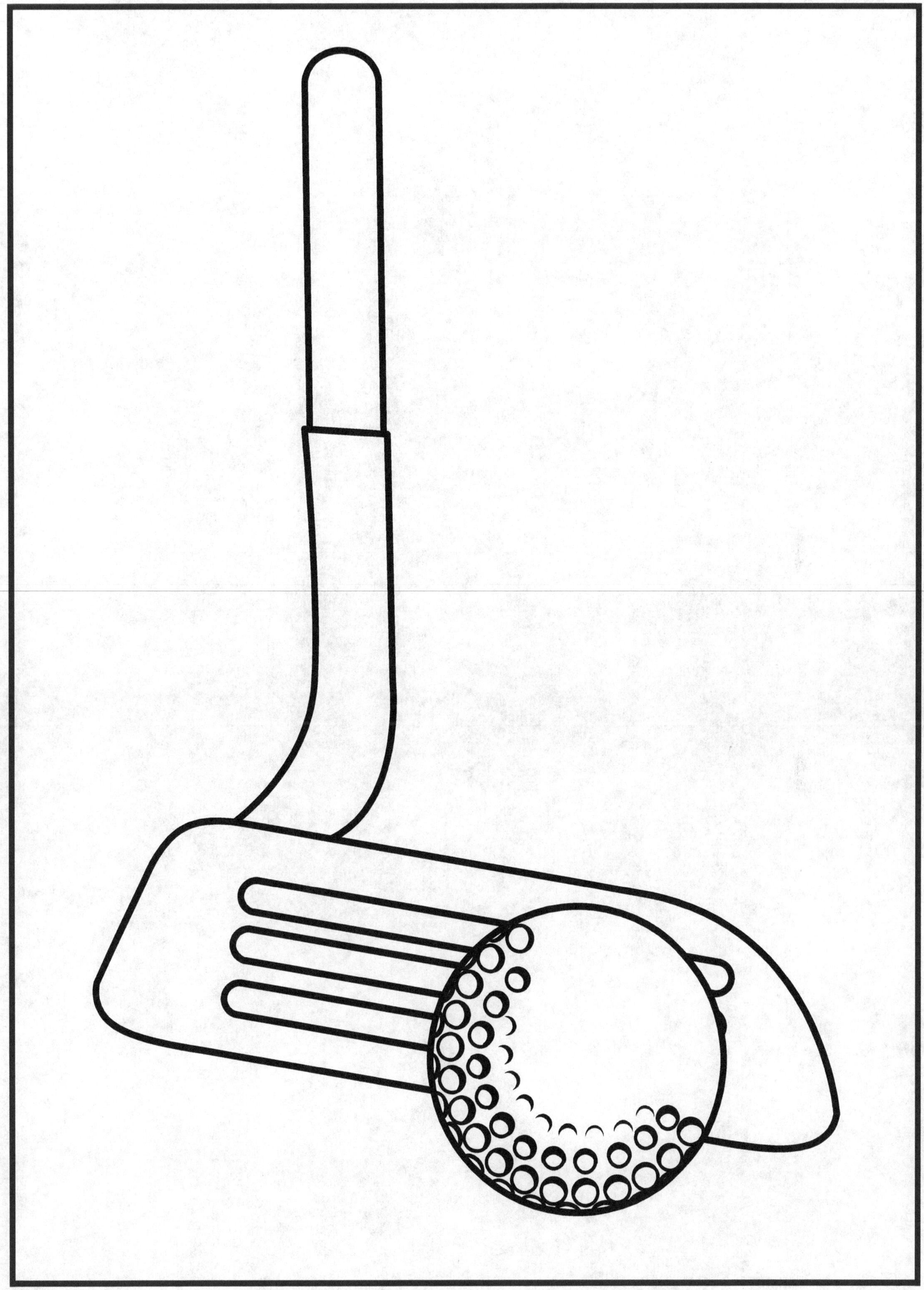

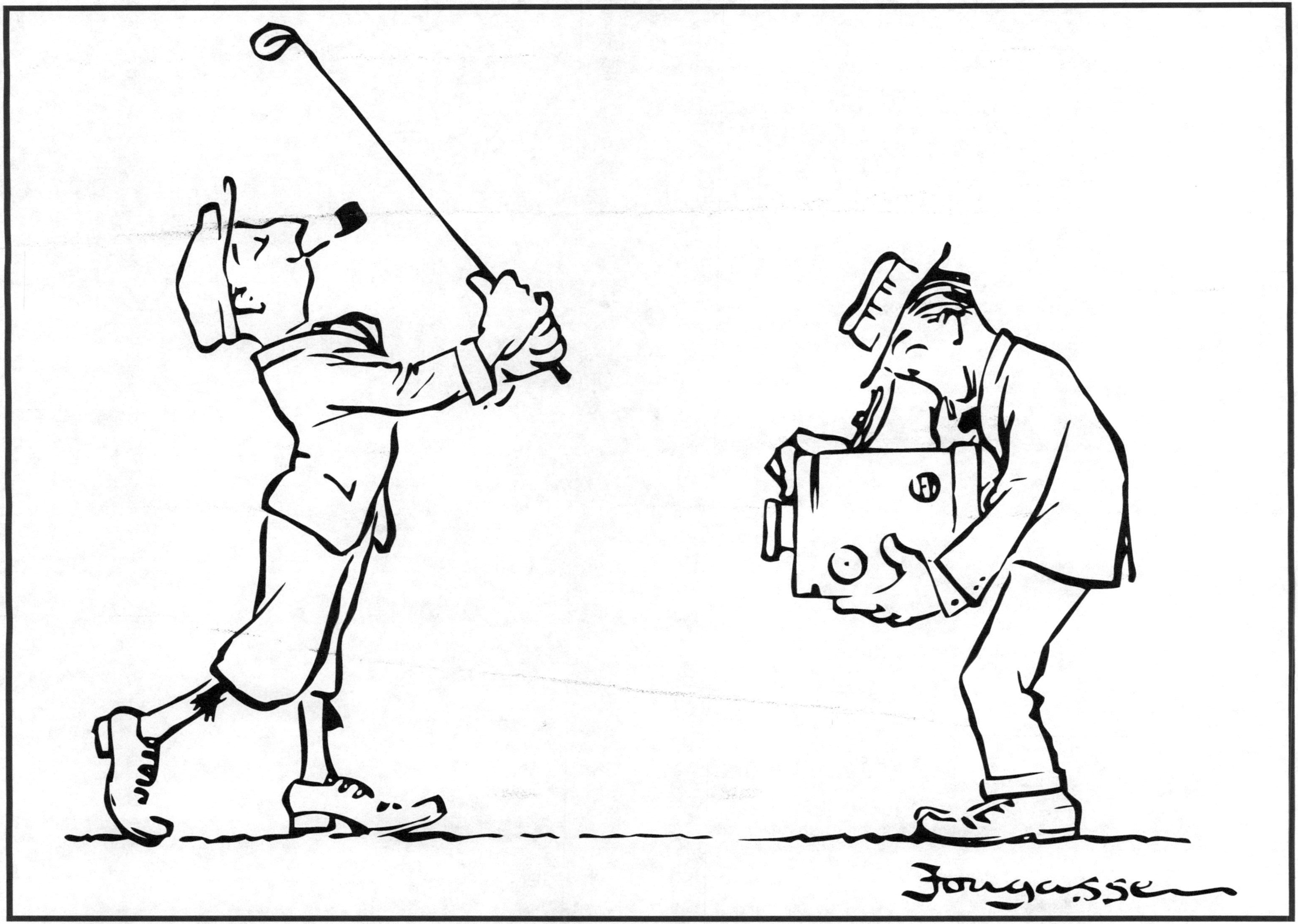
Fougasse

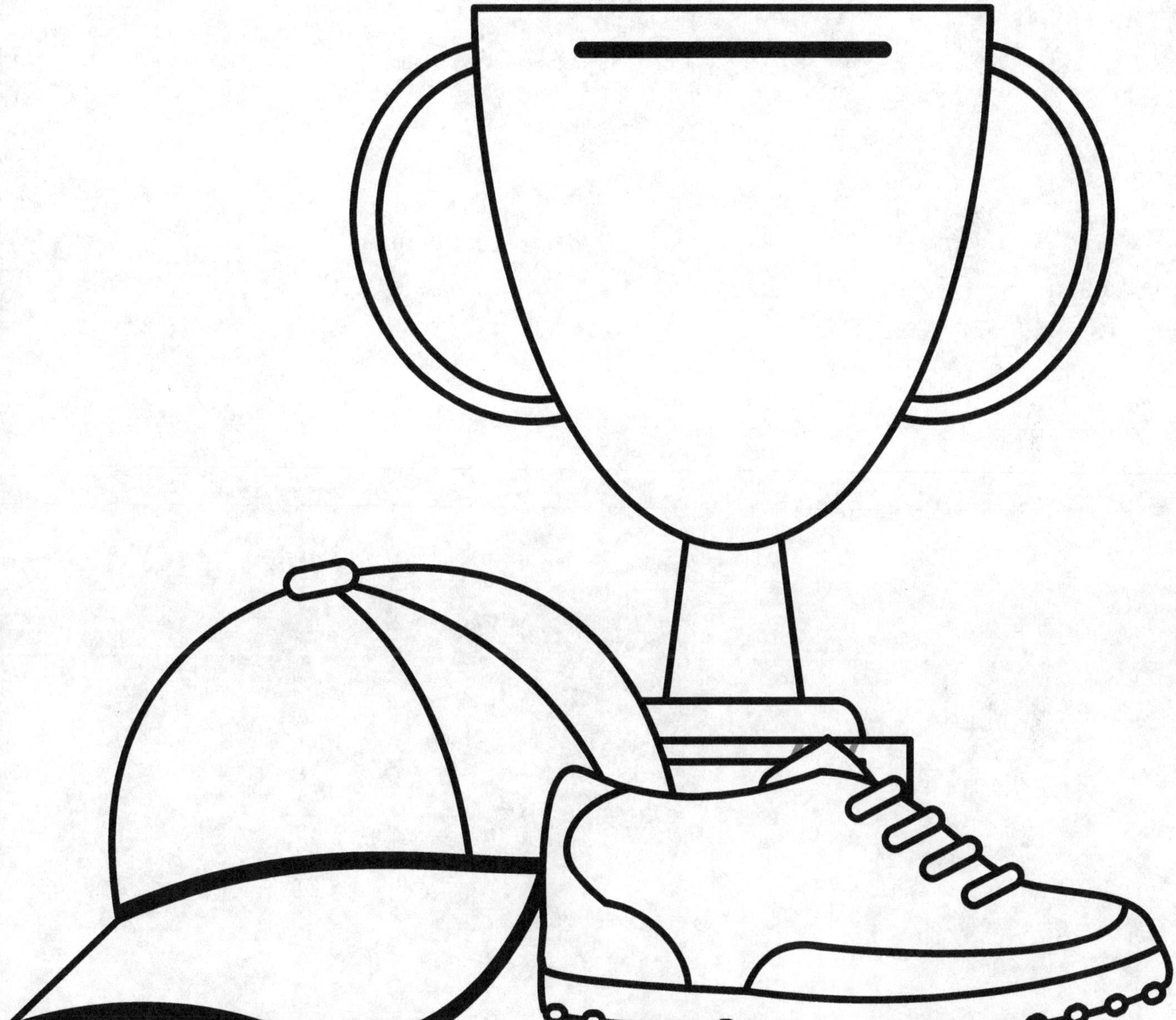

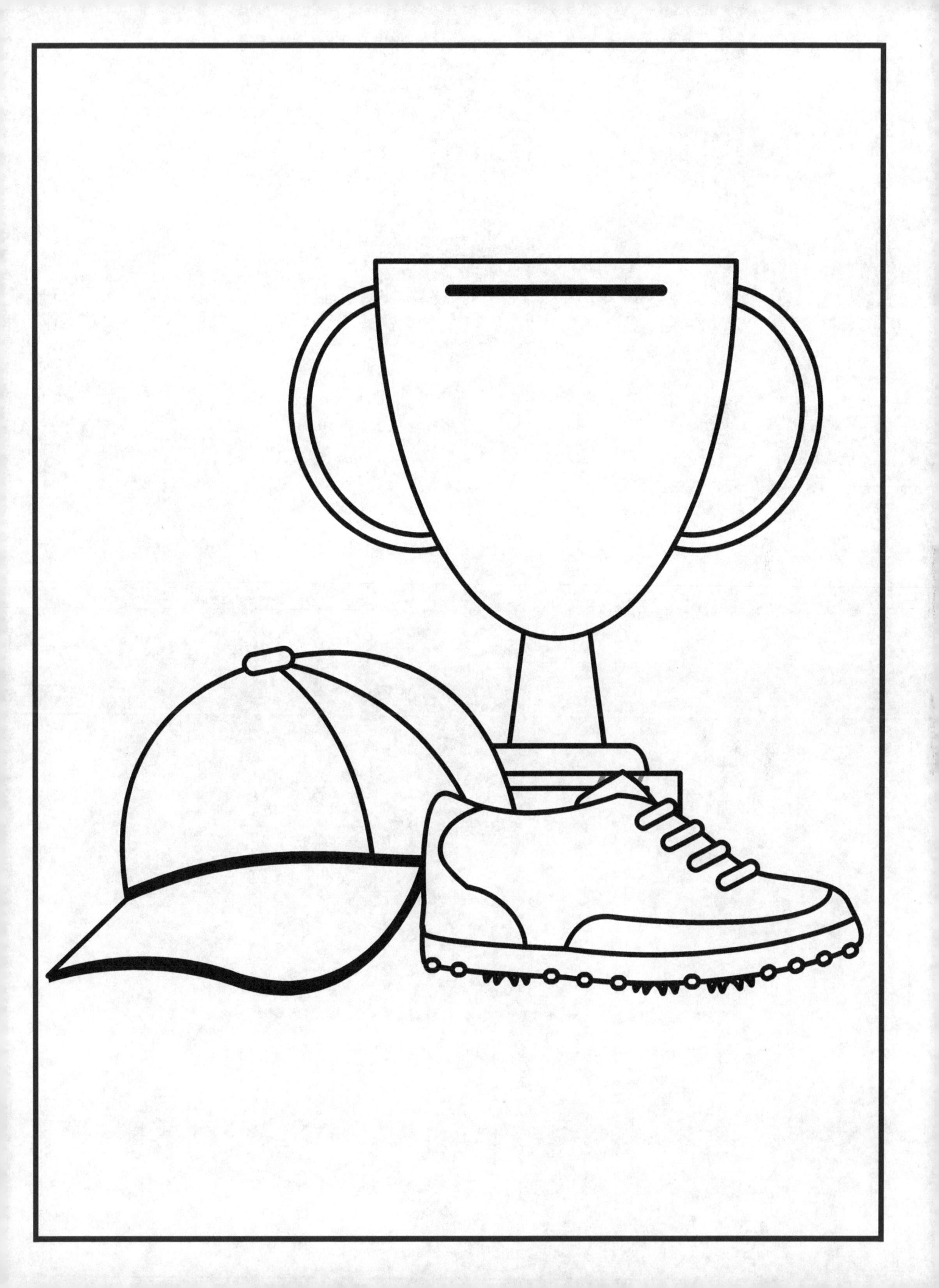

Made in United States
Troutdale, OR
04/14/2025